Learning and Teaching in the Early Years

Playing and exploring

A practical guide to how babies and young children learn

by Anni McTavish

Contents

Published by Practical Pre-School Books, A Division of MA Education Ltd, St Jude's Church, Dulwich Road, Herne Hill, London, SE24 0PB.

Tel: 020 7738 5454

www.practicalpreschoolbooks.com

© MA Education Ltd 2013

Design: Alison Cutler **fonthill**creative 01722 717043

All images © MA Education Ltd. All photos taken by Lucie Carlier with the exception of page 54 (right) taken by Ben Suri; pages: 2, 6, 9, 16-17, 20- 22, 27, 32, 35-37, 39, 40, 47, 54 (left), 56, 61 and main front cover image taken by Anni McTavish; pages 33-34 taken by Tricia Grimes; page 58 taken by Clare Richmond; pages 63-66 taken by Di Chilvers.

ISBN 978-1-907241-37-6

Foreword

Focusing on learning and teaching in the early years

Anyone with children's best interests at heart will agree upon the crucial importance of experiences over the earliest years. However, good intentions are not enough to champion young learners. During early childhood, genuinely helpful adult behaviour – 'teaching' – looks very different from the version that suits older children and the classroom environment.

Those adults, who make a real difference, are knowledgeable about child development and committed to a warm relationship with individual children and their families. They are also confident to be led by young children's personal time frames and learning journeys. They pay close attention to the current

interests of young girls and boys and their enthusiasm for further discoveries.

The authors of this informative series close the gap of meaning that can exist between familiar phrases and a full understanding of what the words mean in best early years practice.

Anni McTavish highlights the central importance of playful experiences for young children's learning. The detailed descriptions support readers to understand how the value of play rests upon respect for babies' and children's own purposes.

By Jennie Lindon, early years consultant

Introduction

About the series

This book is one of a series of three

- **Playing and exploring**

- Active learning

- Creating and thinking critically

The starting point for all three books is that babies and young children are already, from birth, creative and competent thinkers and learners – actively involved in their play and gathering information, ideas and knowledge to build their development and learning.

The youngest babies and children are able to use most of the same strategies that will support them as learners all their lives, such as imitating others, playing with things and finding patterns in their experience so they can predict what will happen. These books unpack how children learn and how adults can best support them in being and becoming learners for life.

Playing and exploring, active learning and **creating and thinking critically** are key characteristics of how children learn and have been linked in recent developmental psychology research to the concept of 'self-regulation'. Self-regulation involves attitudes and dispositions for learning and an ability to be aware of one's own thinking. It also includes managing feelings and behaviour. Self-regulation underpins learning across all areas, developing from birth and supporting lifelong learning (Bronson, 2000).

All babies and young children are different so there is no 'one size fits all' way to foster these characteristics of learning. Young children respond to, and join in with, experiences in different ways depending on a host of factors, including their temperament and the opportunities they have already had. However, the essential message of this book, and the others in the series, is that children (and their families) are entitled to

practitioners who are open to learning from the children with whom they work and who:

- Provide emotional warmth and security

- Tune-in to each unique child by observing and interacting sensitively

- Use observation and knowledge of child development to assess where children are in their learning and plan for next steps and challenges.

All three books provide many illustrative case studies and examples of real-life encounters with children's **active learning**, their **play and exploration** and their **creative and critical thinking**. All these examples demonstrate practitioners and children engaged together in supporting and extending children's learning.

Introduction

The characteristics of children's development and learning were embedded in previous English frameworks and recognised in the commitments, which uphold the principles of the EYFS. The Tickell review (2011) of the EYFS drew on recent research and evidence from practitioners and academics across the early years sector in re-emphasising and highlighting those commitments as the **characteristics of effective learning** and they are an important part of the revised EYFS (2012).

As we look at the three characteristics and the underlying aspects of each one, it is important to remember that they are all interlinked. So imagine that the grid below is like a child's piece of weaving, where they have carefully woven individual strands one way and then another so that they are criss-crossing. This is how it should look and is, in reality, how all children develop and learn.

The three characteristics emphasise **how** babies and young children go about the business of learning, rather than simply focusing on **what** they learn.

How children develop and learn is about the way in which they grow as thinkers and learners and involves them developing learning dispositions such as: curiosity, persistence, concentration, motivation, confidence and excitement. It is about becoming an independent thinker and learner who is able to make decisions and choices and interpret their ideas and solve problems.

Practitioners should find these examples useful when reflecting on their own practice and the early years framework with which they work. The books focus particularly on the English Birth to Five framework: the Early Years Foundation Stage (EYFS), but the characteristics of effective early learning are not tied specifically to any one cultural frame of reference and we hope practitioners working with other frameworks will find the discussion of learning – and the ways in which adults support it – transcends national boundaries.

The characteristics of effective learning

Playing and exploring			
Engagement	Finding out and exploring	Playing with what they know	Being willing to 'have a go'
Active learning			
Motivation	Being involved and concentrating	Keeping on trying	Enjoying achieving what they set out to do
Creating and thinking critically			
Thinking	Having their own ideas	Making links	Choosing ways to do things

> **The starting point for all three books is that babies and young children are already, from birth, creative and competent thinkers and learners – actively involved in their play and gathering information, ideas and knowledge to build their development and learning.**

If children have all these internal 'tools' at their fingertips as well as a good dose of self-confidence, well-being and resilience then **what** they learn will be encountered in a much more meaningful and enjoyable way.

What children learn is about the actual content or knowledge, so, for example, in the EYFS in England this is the **prime** and **specific** areas of learning – although there are many crossovers, particularly between the content of Personal, Social and Emotional Development and the characteristics. All learning is underpinned by social and emotional development. Generally we can see the **what** of children's learning, or the content, as being like the bricks of a building with the **how** children learn and their social and emotional development as the cement and foundations – without which everything would topple over. The rest of this book explains this in much more depth across the age range from babies to children in school.

Just as the characteristics are woven together, so the three books in this series link together.

For example, in Chapter one, there is a shared case study about Jago as he plays with a box of balls. Each book looks at Jago's experience and learning from the different perspectives of **active learning**, **playing and exploring** and **creating and thinking critically**.

Throughout all three books there are further case studies, observations, suggestions for supporting children's language development, reflection points and recommended reading.

About this book

Playing and exploring looks in depth at what is meant by playing and exploring for babies and young children. It considers the developmental theory behind play and how this links to good practice. Each aspect of playing and exploring is unpicked in terms of what it involves, how it can be observed and developed in practice. The book includes:

- Planning and creating a rich, well-resourced learning environment for playing and exploring.

- Why playing and exploring is important for babies and young children's learning and development with examples to show best practice in action.

- Insight and ideas to support practitioners to follow children's interests and extend learning through play and playful interactions.

- Involving parents in their children's play and learning, and how you might improve practice in this area.

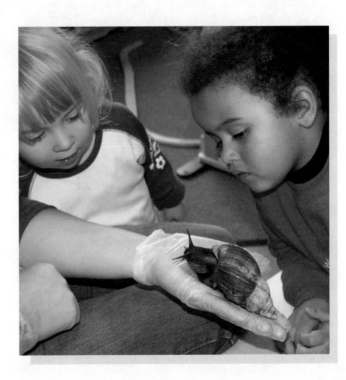

Chapter 1:
What does 'playing and exploring' mean?

The characteristic **playing and exploring** has a fundamental role in children's learning. As they play and explore, babies and young children **engage** with their world, incorporating different strands of learning through their social, emotional, linguistic, physical and sensory development.

Playing and exploring emphasises a child's agency – their growing ability to make choices and decisions and have influence and impact on their environment and others. Through play, children become aware of what they know and what they do that helps them to become successful learners. Together with active learning and creating and thinking critically, it is a key characteristic of lifelong learning.

The qualities that can be nurtured as children engage with their surroundings – imagination, persistence, flexibility and self-confidence, to name but a few, will be essential attributes for the future in our rapidly changing world.

The urge to play and explore is something we share with other mammals – this is particularly true of children and young mammals – we are born with the desire to discover, try-out, create and experiment. A baby begins to explore through their senses and bodily movements and in response to close, loving adults. As they develop mobility, those objects that are often closest to reach – spectacles, a necklace or a bunch of keys all provide fascinating play materials.

Babies, toddlers and children engage in playing and exploring in their own unique way. Play happens on a universal scale, but different cultures may interpret and value play differently (Brooker, p.27, 2010). As early years' practitioners, we need to continue to develop our skills of observation, so we are aware of the different ways children engage in the environment, and value the diverse themes that children can bring to their play.

Children will be learning in other ways too – including being directly taught how to do something, such as: baking biscuits; copying and imitating something they have seen;

gleaning information from books and stories; participating in an adult-led activity or joining-in a discussion about how something works. And, of course, not all play is rich in learning, particularly when it becomes repetitive or stuck-in a-rut and there is not enough adult interaction and support to help it develop and move-on. It is important that we include opportunities for all these different routes to learning, and understand how the characteristic of playing and exploring is an essential tool that will contribute to best possible outcomes for babies, toddlers and young children. The characteristic of **playing and exploring** is divided into three strands:

- **Finding out and exploring**

- **Playing with what they know**

- **Being willing to 'have a go'.**

These are outlined below, with examples of what they might look like in practice.

Playing and exploring – engagement

Aspect of Playing and exploring	What this means	What this might look like
Finding out and exploring	Babies and children show curiosity about objects, events and people. Use their senses to explore the world around them. Engage in open-ended activity. Show particular interests.	A baby touches a cup half-full with cold water. She moves her fingers inside to the surface of the liquid. Lifting them out, she puts her fingers in her mouth. Slowly she puts her fingers back into the cup and then plunges her hand in. Entranced, she discovers the water makes a 'sloshing' sound when she moves her hand up and down.
Playing with what they know	Children pretend objects are things from their own experience. Represent their experiences in play. Take on a role in their play. Act out experiences with other people.	Samir has recently been to his friend's birthday party. He makes a cake with the play-dough and decorates it with glitter and small pieces of straw for 'candles'. He sings Happy Birthday over and over again and blows his candles out.
Being willing to 'have a go'	Children initiate activities. Set and seek their own challenges. Show a 'can do' attitude. Willing to take a risk, engage in a new experience and learn by trial and error.	Joshua watches his older sister tie the laces on her new shoes. Each morning he pulls on his shoes and wraps and twists the laces round and round. He experiments with making a loop and threading the other lace through. He pulls, but both laces come undone. He tries again.

(Reference: Development Matters 2012)

Theory in practice

What 'playing and exploring' means for babies and young children

Babies and young children first and foremost need warm, caring relationships with practitioners who are really interested in their learning and development. They need a well-organised, richly resourced environment with a variety of open-ended materials to explore. Home-based or a group setting, young children will feel secure with a clear routine and structure to their day, with plenty of opportunities to initiate play, as well as participate in adult-supported or adult-led activities. Playful companionship, thoughtful, well-timed questions and thinking ahead for next steps for learning will be part of your adult role. The ethos and atmosphere that supports children's playing and exploring should focus on building on what babies and young children already know, with observation a key tool.

When children are enabled to follow their interests, set their own challenges, to make decisions and reflect on their learning it gives them the best opportunity to develop into **self-regulated** learners.

A self-regulated learner is a child who is motivated (an active learner) and wants to learn. They are curious and interested to find out about things. They are able to 'get going' – decide what they want to do and confident to have a go. This means that not only are they learning practical things like being able to tie their shoelaces, how to socialise and develop cognitive skills (i.e. memory, concentration and reasoning), they are most importantly **learning how to learn**. These skills of being a 'good learner' develop when young children have the opportunity to solve problems, make choices and think about how to overcome a difficulty (creating and critical thinking). This in turn means that children are learning to persevere, and try again, even if something doesn't work first time round.

This emphasis on becoming a self-regulated learner is reflected in the opening paragraph of the revised EYFS (2012) document:

'(Good parenting and) high quality early learning together provide the foundation children need to make the most of their abilities and talents as they grow up'.

And recognises the importance of play as a process for making this happen:

'Play is essential for children's development, building their confidence as they learn to explore, to think about problems, and relate to others'.

All three characteristics of effective teaching and learning are important, but it is through playing and exploring that children develop as active learners and creative and critical thinkers. The key points below highlight how playing and exploring is complex and multi-layered:

- Children may play together with other children or an adult, alongside another, or on their own

- Space and time is essential for children's play and exploration

- Where possible, children will decide the pace and length of time for activities

- Both children and adults will make and learn from their mistakes

- Children will choose activities and will be learning through first-hand experiences

- Self-concept and self-confidence will develop through play

- Play and exploring will enhance brain development

- Children will test out theories, skills and ideas through playing and exploring

- Children may explore fears and anxieties through their play

- Informed adults will evaluate how they plan for different learning styles, and how children can change the environment to suit.

Adapted from Effective Practice: Play and Exploration EYFS 2008. The Practice cards 4.1, 4.2 and 4.3 from the 2008 EYFS English document will still be relevant and together with the new Development Matters 2012 will be a useful reference.

Not every experience or activity within early years can be classed as play – for example a child could be said to be playing if she decides to paint – she chooses the paper, her colours, how to combine them, and for how long. However, the same activity becomes a different experience, if she is asked by her key person to paint a picture of the trees outside the classroom on white paper and is only given twenty minutes to do so.

The difference between playing and exploring

Exploring

Babies and young children will explore and find out about different objects and materials, discovering 'what is this, what is it like?'. They will use all their senses – sight, sound, smell, taste, touch and, as Elinor Goldschmied described, 'the sixth sense of bodily movement' (p.97, 2004). This means that the whole body is attuned and directed towards the exploration – even the baby's toes will be curling and responding. (See the example on page 22 with the baby exploring the curtain tie in Chapter 2). The treasure basket and heuristic play provide ideal opportunities for exploring, and support the development of skills such as concentration and decision making.

This type of activity links to Piaget's (Pound, p.37, 2005) concept of the sensorimotor stage of development from birth to two years of age, when babies and young children's knowledge and understanding is mainly acquired through their physical actions and senses. These early explorations will contribute to later play experiences. Exploring does not stop as we get older, though

it will become more sophisticated, as we bring our previous knowledge and experiences to it.

Playing

When babies and young children are playing, behaviour can be described as playful, imaginative and creative. It involves working out 'what can I do with this object and what can it become?'. Playing is a natural progression from exploring.

In play a child will make their own choices, motivated from within, rather than in response to any outside incentives. A child will be actively engaged, spontaneous, with the focus on the 'doing', rather than any end product. "If the end product is more important than the actual playing, it is unlikely to be real play." (Sue Rogers, Conference 'How Children Learn', 2011.)

However, children may have a goal in mind, and may need your help to achieve it. Playing is more about the way we approach an activity, an attitude and a way of thinking. It will include fantasy and symbolic play – this links to Piaget's preoperational stage of development from two to seven years of age, where children affect the environment and play with ideas (Pound, p.37, 2005). Sue Rogers (conference as above) also reminds us that playing is a feeling as well as many other things. Not only do we learn as we play, but the experience of playing is often pleasurable and makes us feel better. One child said "I

Reflecting on childhood experiences of play can reconnect us with what it means to play and explore. Consider a positive experience of your own when you were playing or exploring – what did you enjoy? Was it energetic, exciting, physical play with a group, or perhaps something quieter, on your own or with another?

- What qualities do you think made it positive? For example, were you outdoors, away from adults and able to choose what and how to play?

- Did you lose track of time or perhaps test your skills and take some risks?

- Were you doing something you had never done before, or repeating a familiar and favourite game?

- What things do you think you might have been practicing or learning about?

- How do you 'play' now as an adult?

like pretending...and being with my friends" and a ten year old described "I feel imaginative...happy (though not if there's an argument), excited – I feel I can do or be anything!".

Another way of looking at these differences has been described in the following way by Hutt et al. 1989 (in 'Free Play in Early Childhood', a literature review NCB, 2007).

Epistemic play – children explore the physical properties of materials and objects, finding out all there is to know about them.

Games with rules – an example of this type of play can be seen in a familiar scenario when a toddler carries a small group of objects back and forth to their familiar adult (they may or may not let you hold the objects!) The game is back and forth, the rule is that the adult smiles, says thank-you and hands back the object.

Ludic play – through this, children find out what they can do with the materials and objects they have explored, and it can involve imagination, fantasy, pretend play, repetition and exaggeration.

Theoretical terms like these provide early years practitioners with a specific language to describe particular behaviour, and can help us to make connections between our ideas for good practice with the theory to back them up. One of my struggles as a practitioner was justifying to parents why we were 'playing again...' or not 'teaching writing just yet...'. Having to answer these questions made me realise I had to find out more about children's learning and development, as well as think of creative and positive ways to share this information with parents. (There are some useful ideas about displays and working together with parents in Chapter 5.)

The 12 features of play

Tina Bruce (2001) identified the following features of play, and suggested that at least half of these must be present for quality play to be taking place:

1. Using first-hand experiences
2. Making up rules
3. Making props
4. Choosing to play
5. Rehearsing the future
6. Pretending
7. Playing alone
8. Playing together
9. Having a personal agenda
10. Being deeply involved
11. Trying out recent learning
12. Coordinating ideas, feelings and relationships for free-flow play.

'Free-flow' play is the term used by Bruce to describe the particular characteristics of open-ended, child-initiated play (not directed, led or influenced by an adult), where the participants can 'wallow in ideas, feelings and relationships' and become more aware of what they know. This growing awareness of 'what you know' (touched on at the beginning of this chapter) and the strategies you employ for learning and how to control it is known as metacognition.

Children will enjoy free-flow play without any adult involvement, as well as other forms of play and exploration, which will be just as valid and provide potential learning experiences. Free-flow play combined with other types of playful activities across a busy day will give children the chance to let off steam, relax and process their learning experiences. Although not directly involved, the adult has an essential and important role, including planning time for free-flow play and the provision of equipment and resources and how they are organised. The other essential role is maintaining and clarifying rules and boundaries for behaviour, use of equipment and safety. Free-flow play is not about a 'free-for-all'.

The Scrapstore PlayPod project™ is one example of how primary aged school children were provided with a rich variety of recycled resources and materials to enhance free-flow play during lunchtimes. The open-ended materials are stored in a giant lorry container that opens up like a wonderful Aladdin's cave of possibilities. Children gather what they need, and play together. Both adults and children reported enhanced playtimes and learning through this provision (www.childrensscrapstore.co.uk).

Time to play and explore

At De Bohun School in the London Borough of Enfield, Anna Ephgrave the reception teacher has planned the daily routine to allow for as much time as possible for children to play and explore – 'We organise the day to maximise the periods of sustained uninterrupted play to encourage in-depth exploration' (p.11, 2011). Her experience has shown that as they have reduced the amount of small group teaching or whole class teaching, children's attainment in all areas has grown. Her approach to child-led learning is well documented in her interesting book 'The Reception Year in Action' 2011.

- How is your timetable and routine planned to allow children uninterrupted time to play and explore?

Playing and exploring for babies

Babies need plenty of close and loving contact with adults who know them well. The key person system (ideally with a co-key person in place for back-up should the main key person be away) will support this adult and child play together. For babies, playing and exploring is about a balance of mainly familiar, with just a few new experiences. When babies are not being held and cuddled, they need a variety of different play opportunities including:

- Ample time on the floor to move and stretch with you close by

Links to practice

- Consider the twelve features of play and take time to observe a child in your setting. Could it be described as 'free-flow'?

- What features do you feel are present in the piece of play you observe?

- Think about any changes that you could make that might increase the quality of play? For example, are there particular resources that you could add to increase the child's explorations, or perhaps the length of time for the play could be extended?

Links to practice

- Take a moment to observe the babies and children you care for.

- How do some children engage with and make choices in the environment – what examples do you spot of epistemic, games with rules or ludic play?

- What do you notice about children's different approaches to the same activities?

- Reciprocal games of peek-a-boo, songs, rhymes and stories

- Playing together with stacking cups, small blocks and musical instruments

- Baby gyms and treasure basket play

- Other rich sensory experiences with time outdoors, safe malleable materials and water play. (Recipes in the appendix for play-dough and an easy 'jelly' made from cooked corn-flour.)

Much of the day for babies is taken up with routines for meals, naps and changing nappies – and these are all opportunities for playful interactions and exploration.

Chapter 1: What does 'playing and exploring' mean?

Playing and exploring for toddlers

Although toddlers are more mobile than babies, they still need plenty of close adult company and companionship. Physical activity and exploration is important. Toddlers will be keen to try things out and experiment, but will want to know you are there to come back to for cuddles and reassurance. They enjoy trying new things and finding out what they can do with a rich variety of different resources.

Like babies, they particularly enjoy repetition – from a simple piece of play to requests for you to sing favourite songs or read stories again and again! They will enjoy playing with sand, water and safe messy play materials. Plenty of time outdoors will allow them to experience the weather, a pile of leaves, watch trees blowing in the wind and the world go by. All children should have some time to connect and play with their brothers or sisters if they are in the same setting. Toddlers will also enjoy playing simple role-play games with their close adult and playing alongside other children.

Playing and exploring for children from three onwards

Children will be developing relationships and making the transition to playing with each other, rather than spending more time playing with adults. They will have particular interests, and pay attention to new ideas too – they are often keen to ask 'why?' questions.

Playing with others requires emotional security, so some children may need extra support and encouragement to do this. Developing language and children's ability and confidence to express their thoughts and feelings is vital.

An important aspect of this age is learning and practicing how to get on with others. Children need to try-out their problem-solving skills by dealing with conflicts and learning about different points of view. Children of this age will really benefit by having time to engage in more detailed play scenarios to develop their ideas, with sensitive adult support and follow-up through short, adult-led groups. (For more on this see the example of the 'whatever you want it to be place' on page 43 in Chapter 3.)

Developmental stages of play

Linking to Hutt's (1989) distinctions between playing and exploring, play is often described by researchers in the following five developmental stages:

> **Children need to try-out their problem-solving skills by dealing with conflicts and learning about different points of view.**

1. **Physical Play** – where babies and infants from birth to six months plus will experiment with bodily sensation and motor movements, with objects and people

2. **Play with objects** – for example, a nine-month old baby will explore objects in a treasure basket

3. **Symbolic play** – pretend play where one thing stands for another, for example a toddler may use a small wooden block to be a mobile telephone

4. **Socio-dramatic** – imaginative, pretend play. Role play in the home-corner, small world, outdoor superheroes

5. **Games with rules** – children will organise shared activities and goals. They will sort out different 'sides' and 'winners' – friendships and hierarchies will be developing through this type of play.

These five types of play frequently cross over each other, and the opportunities you provide for quality play in your setting will contain elements of them all. The babies in the example opposite are exploring their environment through physical play. All the different stages of play feature in the example 'block-play' on page 40.

Play stages

Babies and young children move through different phases of play as they develop socially, initially playing on their own, then alongside another and later in a group.

These stages are categorised in the following way:

Case study – Enhancing child-initiated play

In the baby room at Pastures Way Nursery School, two babies discover the gap in the middle of the floor-standing easel, taking it in turns to crawl through this small space. These two and other infants also enjoy sitting inside the mirror triangular – socialising and playing peek-a-boo.

Baby-room staff respond to these ongoing interests by planning several different den spaces, including a tepee play tent. This sturdy resource had been put to very good use over a number of weeks during my visits to the centre. I first noticed it in the family room, set up with books and musical instruments ready for parents and young children. The next week it was being used by the rising threes and toddlers as part of an exciting space for exploring in and out and enclosures. (See the example on page 51, in Chapter 4 'Willing to have a go in the dark.)

In the baby room, the tepee has been positioned so that the babies can walk or crawl all around the outside, as well as enter in. The mirror triangle is draped with lengths of fabric suspended from the wall, changing a familiar resource into something new and exciting.

The babies are intrigued by these new play opportunities, going around and inside the tepee and back and forth through the triangle.

The adults are close by, attentive to each individual child's needs.

At one point, a practitioner crawls inside the tepee, and smiling and talking to her key child, encourages her to come in. Sitting inside together, another child joined them and they look at several books and play peek-a-boo through the window with a child outside.

After lunch, some cardboard boxes draped with silky scarves have been added to the play possibilities.

- **Solitary play** – the child plays apart from other children, usually with objects or toys that are different from those other children are using. Their attention is mostly centred on their own activity.

- **Parallel play** – A child will play side by side with another, and do similar things. They are aware of and attentive to the other child or children close by. They may also engage in 'parallel speech', where they talk about something similar to the other play, or seem to describe their play/thinking for the benefit of the other children.

- **Associative play** – children begin to play with each other, but in a very loosely organised way. It may involve a slightly more mature or confident child taking the lead, with other children simply following.

- **Cooperative play** – children play together and interact with each other, often with a common purpose or goal. Although different children may be following another's lead, they will exchange ideas, and communication is key.

It is important to recognise that different children will move through these stages at different rates. Children's own personalities and life experiences will influence this.

The new 'Development Matters' document (2012) will help you gather information about the likely behaviours you might expect to see at different ages, with guidance to support and enhance play and learning. In the example above, both solitary and parallel play overlap.

Good practice – observation, assessment and planning

Planning in the here and now

You will be operating on different points in time with your planning – short, medium or long term. The practice example above illustrates the 'in the moment' short-term plan for the babies' exploration and play of different dens and spaces. The practice example on pages 16-18 shows short, medium and long term plans to support babies and toddlers physical development in the under-two's movement session Wiggly Jigglers.

Using the three-stage planning cycle of **observation, assessment and planning**, we can see how the baby room practitioners above developed the children's play.

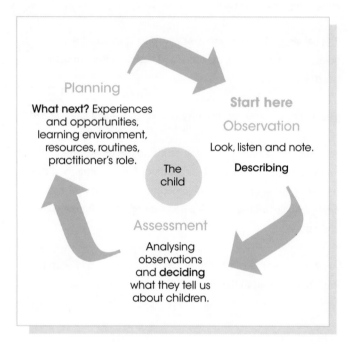

Planning

What next? Experiences and opportunities, learning environment, resources, routines, practitioner's role.

The child

Start here

Observation

Look, listen and note.

Describing

Assessment

Analysing observations and **deciding** what they tell us about children.

Observation

Practitioners observe that the two babies have discovered they can crawl through the easel space, and enjoy and are excited by this.

Assessment

The babies are interested in going back and forth – so likely next steps in the assessment process would be to think about some of the following:

- They seem pleased to have discovered this new activity – would they enjoy other (new) small spaces to explore?

- What do we have already, that can be altered to give a different experience? For example, the triangle was changed by draping different fabrics around it.

- Particular developmental needs – these young babies are at the solitary and parallel stages of play, so a good practitioner

would consider 'I need to provide enough small resources or toys for them to have one each, and they will also enjoy having similar items' and 'there needs to be enough space for them to play alongside each other, but not be too crowded' For example, the practitioner made sure she put a small selection of board books in the tepee, rather than just one.

- Are there any safety issues that need to be taken into consideration?

  - The tepee was placed so that all the babies could crawl or toddle safely around the outside, within easy reach of practitioner help or assistance.

  - The fabric drapes were securely fastened above children's head height with no loose cords or ties.

Planning

Two larger den spaces are planned straight away for the next morning, with room for all the babies to access them easily. These are enjoyed by all the babies in the room, in different ways. Having observed and assessed the mornings play, another den is added, this time made of cardboard boxes, which have very helpfully been left behind by the toy library!

Short, medium and long-term plans will help you to think about and organise opportunities for playing and exploring for all. Very appropriately, the short and medium term planning described here is centred on the babies' interests and developmental stages, rather than any pre-determined, adult-led activity. Adults are involved, crucially, through their playful interactions and in following the children's lead.

The short term planning in this example directly responds to the babies' interest in the here and now. Short-term plans may include you adding something (**enhanced provision**) to the resources and equipment already available (your **continuous provision**). Continuous provision and thinking about how you improve or make changes to it will be part of your ongoing, medium or longer term plans. In this case, the enhanced provision was to add the tepee tent to the continuous provision of painting easel and triangle, and think how best to combine the resources to give some new, exciting play elements to explore.

The practitioners were already thinking ahead – their longer term plan – and discussed with me some of their ideas to increase the dens and cosy spaces in the shared outdoor space for babies and toddlers. These future considerations were mirrored and supported by the senior management team, who were also involved in ongoing discussions about how to improve the outdoor environment for the threes to fives to develop imaginative play and exploration.

All practitioners were involved in this long-term plan by observing and contributing their thoughts about how the children use the fixed play equipment, and a long-term plan was devised to make some significant changes to the outdoor area including building a new dwelling to support open-ended playing and role-play.

In her book 'Planning for Effective Early Learning' (p.22, 2011), Jennie Lindon provides a very helpful and valuable guide to planning, and makes an important point that 'planning' is not only about written plans. Although written plans are important, good practice is never about the written format becoming more important than the information it contains!

The example in Chapter 3, page 47 describes one settings approach to planning through children's interests by using **PLODS ~ possible lines of development**, and how they incorporate these interests into their weekly plan (Rainbow Nursery).

An example of an observation format that may help you consider what you have seen and possible next steps for birth-to-threes and threes-to-fives can be found in the **appendices**, together with a tips sheet with suggestions of the sorts of behaviour you might observe that links to the characteristic of **playing and exploring**. These may offer further ideas towards a commentary about the characteristics for parents and transfer to Key Stage 1.

The important point to consider here is how best to provide play opportunities that really do follow children's starting points in learning, as well as offering inspiring new opportunities for play and exploration to challenge thinking (Brooker, p.37, 2011).

Example reflection

- The babies and toddlers in both examples really benefited from the carefully planned opportunities for movement and play. There are no baby walkers, bouncy chairs or 'bumbo' seats (all of which inhibit free movement experiences).

- An important aspect of developmental movement play is that babies from birth should be given a few minutes each day on their tummies, with an adult close by. This can be done easily

Pause for thought

- An understanding of the developmental stages of play together with your knowledge of individual children – their particular needs, interests, and how they are feeling and behaving right now, today, will help you in planning and thinking about appropriate opportunities for playing and exploring.

- Reflecting on how young children respond to these opportunities will then help you plan next steps. One of the exciting things about working with children is that no two days are ever the same! It is quite possible (even though we may have some idea how children might respond to an activity) that they will take you in a completely new direction.

- It can be helpful to take time to reflect how well planning and organising for play experiences works for individual children and the group as a whole.

- But, don't let this put you off planning a particular experience with one or two children in mind. Often the enthusiasm and interest shown by one child is contagious and others will quickly be drawn into the activity.

by having them lie on your chest or stomach or on a soft mat on the floor. This gives them the important experience of practicing lifting their heads. Babies who do not seem to enjoy tummy time (and some won't if they have not had the experience very often) might prefer it on a large soft ball (a Pilates ball is a good idea), or rolled-up towel or cushion. Do this for just a few moments initially, and build up time gradually. (A useful article about the importance of tummy time can be found here: http://news.bbc.co.uk/1/hi/5128144.stm.)

- Tummy time is still important as children get older – think of children you know who prefer to lie on the floor to read, play or watch television. One idea might be to offer a selection of drawing materials laid out on a cloth on the floor.

- These valuable experiences do not rely on expensive equipment – good use has been made of recycled materials.

Case study – Jago and the box of balls

Crawling closer, he stretches forward, pivoting on one knee, with the other leg stretched out for balance. Using his left hand he pulls the ball closer and then brings his right hand in to grasp it firmly.

Success! Jago concentrates on moving the ball back and forth and eventually pulls it over the edge of the box.

In this case study the three strands of **playing and exploring** can be observed.

- Finding out and exploring

- Playing with what they know

- Being willing to 'have a go'.

Links are also made in the text to the other characteristics of effective teaching and learning – **active learning** and **creating and thinking critically**.

It has been a busy morning at Wiggly Jigglers – a creative movement session for under two's and their parents. An arts centre bar in the evening, the space has been organised creatively by the movement specialist Jasmine and a helper to allow for safe play and exploration. The materials have been arranged based on the experiences from the last session, with some new additions – small steps and cushions have been added with a gym mat underneath. From time to time, Jasmine rearranges materials, or moves something closer to a baby and parent.

Jago and his mum are one of the last to leave at the end of the session, and tidying up has begun.

His attention is drawn to a shallow cardboard box full of different sensory balls. Jago watches as a practitioner tidies a ball away into the box.

Crawling closer, he stretches forward, pivoting on one knee, with the other leg stretched out for balance. Using his left hand he pulls the ball closer and then brings his right hand in to grasp it firmly.

Though tired at the end of the morning, Jago is interested to explore more. He is **finding out and exploring**. Innate curiosity fuels this 'hands-on' adventure, helping him to find out about the ball and test his ideas.

- **Active learning** – being involved and concentrating

> *Innate curiosity fuels this 'hands-on' adventure, helping him to find out about the ball and test his ideas.*

The ball rolls across the floor, Jago turns and immediately crawls after it.

Next, one at a time, he rolls two shiny balls over the edge and puts them side-by-side.

- **Creating and thinking critically** – having their own ideas (finding ways to solve problems).

Success! Jago concentrates on moving the ball back and forth and eventually pulls it over the edge of the box.

Does Jago already know that if he keeps on trying, he can get what he wants? **He is willing to 'have a go'** and this helps him to achieve his goal of moving the ball out of the box.

- **Active learning** – keeping on trying

- **Creating and thinking critically** – making links and testing his idea.

The ball rolls across the floor, Jago turns and immediately crawls after it. Jago has initiated this activity. **He is finding out and exploring**, showing particular interests. Even though the ball has rolled away, he pursues it, determined to find out more.

- **Active learning** – enjoying achieving what they set out to do

- **Creating and thinking critically** – choosing ways to do things.

Jago continues to play and explore. He retrieves the red ball, crawls back with it grasped between his thumb and finger and puts it back in the box. Next, one at a time, he rolls two shiny balls over the edge and puts them side-by-side.

Jago's mum has moved closer. She 'tunes-in', sensing his tiredness, but allows him time to carry on exploring. Sensitive adult support enables him to persist in this experience. Eventually, he cries and moves closer to his mum, and she picks him up.

Note

Each book in the Learning and Teaching in the Early Years series shares the same practice example above in Chapter 1, identifying the different strands of the characteristics of effective learning.

Chapter 1: What does 'playing and exploring' mean?

Links to practice

Movement play indoors is a different experience to physical play outdoors and it may be something you plan for already.

Take a moment to sit or lie down on the floor where babies and young children spend their time, and remind yourself what they can see and feel from this vantage point.

Any or all of the following resources will support exploratory movement play:

- Time and a cleared space

- A soft mat or rug

- Fabric, scarves and voile

- Bubble wrap, foil and silver athlete 'blankets'

- Cardboard tubes, a fabric tunnel and a few different size cardboard boxes

- A firm bean-bag, a Pilates ball or space hopper

- Cushions

- Ribbon sticks and lengths of ribbon

- Small bean bags

- Soft and shiny sensory balls

- Egg-shaped music shakers for small hands and short rain-sticks

- An engaged adult who joins in and facilitates the play – rearranges materials if necessary, offers a particular resource and makes sure children are safe in their explorations.

If you were planning the next Wiggly Jigglers session, what opportunities or resources would you make sure were available for Jago? Would you include anything new?

- No adult chairs meant that the adults naturally sat on the floor close by their babies, supported by cushions or a large beanbag.

- There were plenty of the same things, so parents, babies and toddlers did not need to wait for a turn, have to share or get frustrated in their efforts to play if someone had something they wanted.

- All these materials gave rise to rich exploratory movement play, yet we can feel pressured as practitioners and parents to have the 'right' toy or piece of equipment, in order that our children learn 'correctly'.

- Even though the session had finished, Jasmine and her helper did not rush Jago and his mum – they simply began in a relaxed way to tidy-up. Although time-keeping is important, occasionally a few minutes extra 'special time' can benefit a child's explorations and build your relationship with the parent.

Communication and language

This was supported in the following ways:

Sensitive adult support – Jago's mum shows she is interested by sitting nearby, smiling and watching.

Key words – She offers the occasional word or comment – 'shiny', 'the red ball...' or 'you've got it!' This supports Jago's play and provides simple language to match his experience of finding out about the balls.

Keeping quiet – too much chat or questions can be very distracting. The adults spoke quietly and apart from the occasional comment, Jago's mum was quiet.

Mood – Soft music was played from time to time to help create a calm atmosphere during the movement session. At the end, no music is playing and the only sounds are Jago's movements and his mother's voice.

Babies and young children will benefit from a balance of musical experiences and chat, but too much background noise can inhibit language development. (O'Hare N, 'All Ears' from *Listener – the things that matter*, National Literacy Trust, 2006) So, limit the time for recorded music or loud chat, and this will support concentration and allow you to tune into children's own musicality.

Links to areas of learning and development

In the 2008 English EYFS document, the commitments under the theme of learning and development share equal space. The first three commitments are the characteristics of effective learning (practice cards 4.1, 4.2 and 4.3), with the fourth (4.4) being the areas of learning and development. This has now changed in the revised EYFS 2012 document, the characteristics have been given more prominence and the areas of learning and development have been redefined into three **prime** and four **specific** areas.

Prime areas

- Personal, social and emotional development

- Physical development

- Communication and language.

Specific areas

- Literacy

- Mathematics

- Understanding the world

- Expressive arts and design.

The characteristics of playing and exploring, active learning and creating and thinking critically link to other curriculum documents and initiatives in the UK and beyond. For example, the approach in the Italian pre-schools of Reggio Emilia has an emphasis on developing positive learning dispositions through the arts; the High Scope system from America in a similar way focuses on supporting independent, self-regulated learning. It uses a structure called 'plan, do, review' to support children to reflect on their individual learning processes. The work of Dr Ferre Laevers from Belgium and the Leuven Scales of well-being and involvement has been explored and implemented in different settings in this country as a way of assessing children's positive learning characteristics.

Rather like the threads of a spider web, the characteristics of effective learning interweave through and between different areas of learning and development. Jago in the example on pages 16-17 shows many of the characteristics of effective learning. For example:

- He is curious and shows particular interest in the different balls (playing and exploring)

- He is not easily distracted and persists, even though the ball rolls quite far away! (active learning)

- He finds a way to hold on to the ball and brings it back to the box, and this is quite a difficult manoeuvre for a one year old. He achieves his goal to put it back into the box (creating and thinking critically).

All of these statements could be used to describe his play, and form part of a next steps review to plan further opportunities for playing and exploring.

If we were to consider Jago's play by looking at the three **prime** areas the following statements from 'Development Matters' (2012) reflect his learning and development:

Personal, social and emotional development

Self-confidence and self-awareness – Uses pointing with eye gaze to make requests, and to share an interest. Explores new toys and environments, but 'checks-in' regularly with familiar adult as and when needed.

Managing feelings and behaviour – Uses familiar adult to share feelings such as excitement or pleasure, and for 'emotional refuelling', when feeling tired, stressed or frustrated.

Making relationships – Builds relationships with special people. Interacts with others and explores new situations when supported by familiar person.

Communication and language

Listening and attention – Has a strong exploratory impulse. Concentrates intently on an object or activity of own choosing for short periods.

Understanding – Understanding of simple words in context is developing – in this instance 'ball', 'tired?'.

Speaking – Uses pointing with eye gaze to make requests, and to share an interest.

Physical Development

Moving and handling – Sits unsupported on the floor. When sitting, can lean forward to pick up small toys. Crawls, bottom shuffles or rolls continuously to move around. Passes toy from one hand to the other.

Health and self-care – Responds to and thrives on warm, sensitive physical contact and care.

Top 10 tips for playing and exploring

1. De-clutter and organise the environment to be interesting, enticing and accessible.

2. Have regular tidy-ups, reorganise resources, discard broken materials, and arrange materials in new, inviting ways.

3. Provide something new to a familiar activity (for example, if you notice one of your children is interested in balls, provide another of a different size, texture and weight.)

4. Engage in activities and experiences yourself in an exploratory way.

5. If you notice a child is struggling, be on hand to encourage, or with sensitivity, demonstrate how something might work.

6. Plan space, time and a calm atmosphere.

7. Spend time watching and observing how different children play and explore.

8. Be sensitive to opportunities for direct teaching.

9. Plan for possibilities, rather than clear outcomes.

10. Acknowledge, praise and notice a child's efforts, as well as what they achieve.

Chapter 2: Finding out and exploring

Playing and exploring

Finding out and exploring

Playing with what they know

Being willing to 'have a go'

Babies and children instinctively find out and explore right from the word go. Finding out and exploring enables babies and young children to gather the essential ingredients to help them understand and begin to make sense of their world.

They actively seek stimulation and interactions, which build and strengthen the neural pathways in their brain. These vital connections develop through everything that a baby sees, hears, tastes, smells and touches through their physical experiences as they find out and explore. A rich variety of appropriate experiences and activities will aid the healthy development of these connections, and help the brain pare away unused ones.

Very young babies are ready to be social and communicative, and quickly develop a range of strategies to satisfy their needs. Good practitioners will be sensitive and tune-in to these early, non-verbal communications. It is important to recognise that babies and children are also finding out and exploring as they play games like peek-a-boo and experiment with sounds, gestures, gurgles, smiles and other social interactions. Young children change and grow rapidly in the first three years of life – from the non-mobile baby who is reliant on adults to communicate with them and provide them with interesting materials to explore –to the busy toddler often on the move.

Babies and children **find out and explore** when they:

- Use their senses to explore the world around

- Are curious about activities, objects and people

- Show and develop interests

- Participate in open-ended exploration.

Case study: Finding out and exploring with a household object

The curtain tassel is a favourite toy of baby Tao, six-months-old. She brings it with her every day when she attends her childminder's. Tao's mum had given it to her one day at home and since then Tao has been fascinated by it.

She is lying on a soft blanket on the living room floor with her child-minder close by as she helps another child set up a train track. Tao has the end of the tassel tightly grasped between both hands. The tassel has a short loop of soft, twisted rope, which runs through a fabric-covered ring. The tassel itself is made up of lots of tiny threads and it is this part that Tao is interested in at the moment. She moves the tassel slowly back and forth across her mouth, touching the threads carefully with her tongue. She pulls the tassel closer, and part of the rope tugs against her feet –she pushes back with her foot. Her childminder tickles her tummy gently and says 'you like that old rope, don't you Tao?'. Tao gurgles, pushing her other foot again her child-minder's knee in response.

Ordinary household objects like the one in this example can offer rich sensory experiences. The treasure basket is an ideal resource for babies who are sitting up but not yet crawling. Offering a wide variety of different natural materials and objects (nothing plastic) provides young children with wonderful opportunities to find out and explore.

Natural materials – making your own treasure basket

Many treasure baskets are available commercially, but it can be very satisfying to create your own. Your choice of materials will be informed by what you already know about your children's preferences and interests.

Invite parents to contribute – personal items from home make a treasure basket even more special. It can be helpful to have a box of extra bits and pieces, so you can rotate and change objects regularly to offer new experiences.

Gather a variety of objects in a round, shallow basket that does not tip easily, although a small cardboard box free of staples will work just as well.

Suggested items: Large fir-cone, smooth pebbles, shells, small wooden bowl, little tins with lids (some with small object inside

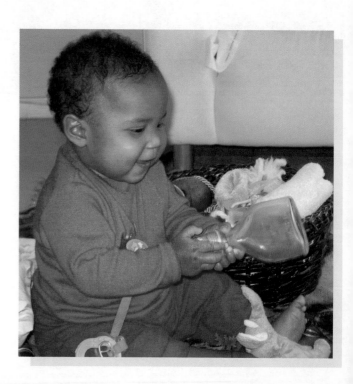

that rattles when shaken), short-handled wooden spoon, whisk, honey stirrer, leather and bead purses, smooth, solid glass bottle, lengths of ribbon, lace, satin fabric, small woven baskets, large feather, small fabric belt, large buckle, giant wooden beads on a string, metal bracelets and bangles, metal cooking measuring cups, large wooden and metal curtain rings, loofah, giant seed pod, small natural maraca shakers or rain stick, jam-jar lids, a soft teddy or knitted animal, kitchen-roll tube, a short length of metal chain (with safe, soldered links), piece of leather, secure bead necklaces, a well-secured lavender bag. A clean washed lemon or orange could also be offered – as long as children do not have skin conditions like eczema that might be irritated by them.

Safety

- The materials should be checked for any damaged or broken edges and cleaned regularly. There is some concern that using household cleaners or sterilising agents can build up over time and affect babies' immune systems. Simple hand washing with either warm slightly soapy water or plain water will suffice; some materials could be put through a dishwasher cycle.

- Always use your common sense on suitability of objects. Nothing should be small enough to get stuck in a child's mouth or cause choking and if you are in any doubt, leave the object out.

- An adult should always be close by and watchful during play, and in shared spaces with different ages, you may need to section off a small area (a low trough book shelf works well or several large cushions) so older children do not bump into the babies.

- If you find that older children consistently show interest in the materials and want to take them off, it is a clear message that they are in need of sensory rich play too! (See heuristic play page 24 and other ideas throughout this chapter).

Sensitive adult support

Plan a time in the day when babies are not tired or hungry. Mid-morning or afternoons when children have had a sleep can work well. Babies have been known to play for up to an hour with treasure basket materials, and once play is finished (remember to remove any fruit) the treasure basket/s should be covered with a clean cloth or tea towel and put away. Different settings offer treasure basket play every day or as and when they feel the babies will enjoy it.

The adult should be present and attentive, but not intrude in the babies' play. You can encourage babies to make their own choices about what they want to explore and for how long. If there are two or three babies playing you will need a well-stocked treasure basket with plenty of materials for all. Some babies will benefit from having you right next to them, as they may need your reassurance that it is alright to explore and discover new things.

Links to practice

- What opportunities are there in your setting for young children to explore natural materials?

- What materials are children particularly interested in? Are some objects real favourites?

- How do children move and explore? Do they do this by mouthing objects, or do they touch and stroke them, twist, turn or bang them on the floor?

- If you were to add something new, what might this be?

- How might you share or involve parents in treasure basket or heuristic play for their child?

- Take photographs of babies playing with treasure basket/heuristic play materials and create a display. You can make links to the characteristics of effective learning – playing and exploring. For example, for baby Tao in the example above, you might say something like: 'Tao is using her senses to explore the curtain tie. She is curious, engaging and showing her interest in open-ended exploration. She is also developing her skills of concentration and decision-making'. Finding out and exploring is the foundation for later problem solving abilities, mathematics and science-based concepts. It would be appropriate to choose several statements from developmental matters in the prime areas (personal, social and emotional, communication and language and physical development) and include these as captions for your display.

Usually you would not talk or chatter whilst babies are at play with the treasure basket, for there are plenty of other opportunities during the day for interactions. However, I would encourage practitioners' to use their professional judgement. If you have a concern about a child's language development for example, playing together and sensitively following their lead in choice of objects and offering some key words might be very helpful.

Heuristic play (meaning to discover and find out about) is the next stage on from treasure basket play and is aimed at the mobile baby and toddler between the ages of one and two. Heuristic play involves having a variety of small materials (shells, pebbles, fire-cones, pom-poms, lids, ping-pong balls, old-fashioned clothes pegs, lengths of chain, ribbon, corks etc) and a selection of different size containers (tins with edges safely covered with tape, small baskets, cardboard drinks tubes, clear plastic tubes, small boxes, plastic water bottles of different size etc.). These materials are arranged attractively in a cleared space in order to encourage lots of exploratory play, the essence of which is 'what can I do with it?'. The preoccupation of this age group is in lots of tipping, filling, emptying and posting. If parents report that children are posting things (i.e. bank cards through floorboards/keys into DVD players!) it might be helpful to suggest planning for some heuristic play at home.

The aim is to provide plenty of materials so there is no need to share, and in a similar way, the focus is on the play, rather than interacting with the children. The adult has a key role in being present and available, noticing how children play and intervening to offer more of a certain material to help a child follow their particular interest.

The materials can either be stored in a large cardboard box or bag, but for larger groups of children it works best to have separate drawstring bags to collect each group of objects into. At least a third of the time you set aside for heuristic play should be spent towards the end involving the children in tidying up. Children of this age often enjoy this, and it helps everyone feel part of the group and have a pleasurable sense of achievement when everything is cleared away.

None of the materials for these types of important exploratory play are expensive, but they are invaluable in giving children under three rich opportunities for finding out and exploring, the 'expense' is in the energy and effort required by creative practitioners to gather and maintain the collections. A very useful reference book is *Developing Play for Under Threes* by Anita Hughes (2010).

In planning for finding out and exploring the **physical environment** matters but so too does the **emotional environment**. This includes the relationships between parents, practitioners and children, the atmosphere that is created and the ethos and beliefs about what constitutes a rich environment for learning for babies and young children. Outdoors provides different opportunities, and play and exploration you have noticed inside can be extended outdoors in exciting, complementary ways. (See the example 'representing experiences through schematic play in Chapter 3, page 45.)

Many children, particularly boys, prefer to be outdoors and in some cases your setting might be the main outdoor experience for them. Being outdoors can help calm high energy levels and is the ideal place for bigger, louder play. It offers children opportunities to learn about nature, plants and taking care of the natural world. Children can experiment; opportunities can be planned for them to use their strength safely and learn through taking appropriate risks. Children learn to be safe and sensible by having the chance to take small risks – this helps them to make appropriate judgements later on to manage larger risks.

Each setting has its own unique strengths and circumstances to work with. Settings that are in shared spaces, and pack away each day or every week, require practitioners to be creative, and think carefully about how to use space to its best advantage.

One childminder I spoke with described her tiny garden, but also the variety of different materials in small quantities that she was able to provide. She had invested in a builder's tray for messy and malleable play, which she used on the ground for shallow water-play for one of her babies or on a low table for messy/malleable play for two school-age children several afternoons a week. The builder's tray was stored behind a small shed when not in use. Indoors, shoe-boxes were stored under the bed and each contained different 'interest collections'. These included: shells and pebbles; spoons of all shapes and sizes; tiny teddy-bears; balls of all different colours, texture and size; a selection of kaleidoscopes; shiny materials including small acrylic mirrors, silver foil, soft fabric stars, tins and lids etc.

An enabling environment

- Plan the day to take into account children's needs and include time for uninterrupted play. Flexibility when children are tired and need quiet time is essential.

- Offer a range of open-ended resources so that children can role-play, use and combine materials in different ways.

- Organise space indoors and out with opportunities for children to explore and repeat activities and experiences they enjoy.

- Plan experiences and challenges that are developmentally appropriate.

- Re-think how to use equipment/resources in novel and different ways, i.e. bring a small climbing frame indoors to make a den. Place art or heuristic play materials on top of a mat or shower curtain on the floor, so children can access them lying down or sitting on small cushions.

- Plan opportunities for children to play and participate with others who are more skilled or experienced, in order to support children learning from each other.

- Consider that children may want to move resources and equipment to suit their explorations and patterns of play.

- Make links with children's interests (including interests at home) – if space travel and rockets fascinate, supply small world astronauts and moon vehicles; silver survival blankets, or cardboard and silver paint.

- Too much colour, light, sound and pattern can be over-stimulating and distressing. This includes loud adult voices. Children need to be able to 'get away from it all' and play undisturbed.

- Take clues from nature for indoor decoration; plan large expanses of colour in soft blues and greens and natural materials. Limit pattern to smaller areas like cushion covers. Plan quiet times before and after lunch.

The quality of experiences we provide for children is important. Rather than too many resources out all at once, which can create an overloaded feeling, it is far better to plan opportunities with depth, time and room to really explore.

Each child will be unique and different in the way they approach activities. Good practitioners will be sensitive to this and model exploring and finding out to those children who are nervous or hesitant. A child who is easily side-tracked may also need your help to slow down and explore more carefully. Applying good practice of observation, assessment and planning will help you decide what opportunities to offer next.

Anna and the treasure basket

Anna and her mum have come to visit. Anna, eight-months-old, is sitting happily playing with the materials in my treasure

> " Rather than too many resources out all at once, which can create an overloaded feeling, it is far better to plan opportunities with depth, time and room to really explore. Each child will be unique and different in the way they approach activities. "

basket, sitting on a warm blanket on the living room floor. She stretches a hand out and grasps a soft, velvet toy elephant, which she mouths, all the while watching her mum, who smiles and calls her name.

Anna then lifts out a small glass bottle with a screw top metal lid. Holding it in both hands she pivots forward

slightly to adjust to the weight of the bottle. Anna's mum notices the bottle and is delighted – she had given it to me several years ago with a group of objects for my treasure baskets. The bottle is special she tells me, because it used to belong to her grandfather. Anna really enjoys exploring it, and when they leave I return the bottle to take with them.

Are there objects or toys that have particular significance for the children and families you care for?

Providing smooth glass objects in a treasure basket for babies may cause some anxiety with other practitioners or parents. They are safe in the hands of babies (who are not yet crawling) – a baby is not yet physically able to throw, and if the object drops onto a soft blanket or rug it very unlikely to break. Glass and metal objects provide a distinctive sensory experience – they are often quite cold when first touched, but take on warmth through being held.

The process of finding out and exploring does not stop as we get older, nor should it be left behind as children leave their earliest years. Opportunities for finding out and exploring should continue through into primary and beyond. This is often the place where friendships between children begin, develop and deepen, with the joint sharing of ideas, collaborations and experiments. Offering plenty of time to explore materials such as dough or clay with different tools gives children the chance to find out about the properties of the material before being

Pause for thought

Involving children in deciding what they would like to know more about or explore next, gives them the message that what they are interested in is valued, and that they have some control over their environment. Confident practitioners will include children in discussions and ideas to change or alter existing provision, as seen in the example below at Hindley's Pre-school.

One way of doing this is to mind-map or involve children in '3D-planning' with coloured plastic hoops, sitting on the floor in a small group. For example, if you observe a group have really enjoyed playing with sand, you would gather a small amount of sand in a bowl and place this in a hoop in the middle of your circle (you might also model writing 'sand' in yellow on a piece of card and add this label to the sand). Three or four other hoops are placed around to contain ideas the children come up with. For example, you might ask:

- What would make the sand more interesting?

- What resources or equipment would make it better?

- Do they have other ideas for games/activities in the sand?

- Would some children like other friends to join their play?

- If there are some children who don't often access the sand, would they play there if a particular resource was added?

You may need to initiate and model an idea or suggestion first, until the children get the hang of this exercise. It is important to follow through with the children's suggestions, and review together how they work.

Practice example from an artist in residence

'As a potter I like to encourage children to explore and experiment with the clay, to see what sort of shapes and patterns evolve. Children who have had plenty of early opportunities to play and explore with clay, play-dough, collage, sticks and stones are invariably more secure to begin immediately working, designing and creating. Those who haven't had that early experience sometimes struggle and need at least a day to get familiar with the clay, how it works and what the possibilities are.' *Ricky Grimes, Ceramic Artist*

expected to make something or use it in a specific way. Although direct teaching of particular skills can be invaluable, it needs to be well-timed with opportunities for children to discover and find things out for themselves. Children who have the chance to do this regularly develop good problem solving skills and build their confidence to come up with creative solutions.

Children and adults planning together for finding out and exploring

At Hindley's Pre-school the outdoor area has developed over time with input and discussion involving children, parents and other members of the community. Much thought and attention to detail has gone into making this a fascinating and rich environment for finding out and exploring. The area used for water play is constantly evolving depending on children's interests at the time. For example a 'water-wall' feature was created after discussing different ideas with the children. This was constructed using a variety of tubes, funnels, plastic bottles and drainpipes, and prompted many questions about how and where did the water go after it 'got down'?

The practitioners were able to extend this child-initiated play with thoughtful adult-led discussions and began a project to find out all sorts of inspiring and different things about water. These conversations are recorded in a special book, with observations, photographs and other information discovered by the children. The head of centre told me this was called their 'Love Book', and this seemed a very apt name for a journal that celebrates all the activities the children love to do!

On the morning of my visit, several children are in the water play space, experimenting with blue paint and water. They have access to a hosepipe and notice that the watery blue paint, once added to the star-fish shape feature on the ground, can easily be 'tracked' in order to find out exactly where it goes (into a small drain in the corner of the space). Some children gather pebbles and stones nearby to add to these experiments, whilst one child brings several dinosaurs to join the play. The star-fish shape on the ground is the latest addition to this area, following a similar joint planning process as described above.

Children are able to help themselves to a snack indoors throughout the morning, which allows them maximum time to continue finding out and exploring. After tidying-up the group comes together late morning for a short movement and relaxation session before sitting down for lunch.

Assessing your environment

Assessing the quality of **finding out and exploring** in your setting and the effectiveness of your environment are important considerations.

In her reception class Anna Ephgrave at De Bohun School works closely with her team to support and develop children's independence (and save adult time for really important interactions) and suggests that a useful way to assess your environment is to look at the different reasons why children approach adults (Ephgrave, p.6, 2011). For example:

● If children often approach adults because they can't find tools or materials, then organisation of materials needs to be considered.

● If they come telling tales or there are squabbles, there needs to be a focus on supporting and developing conflict resolution skills and checking to see if there are enough resources.

● If children ask permission to go to the bathroom regularly or query what they can and can't do, rules and 'what's possible' need to be clarified.

● As new issues arise you can look at what might need to be changed in the environment, or take time to focus on a particular issue of behaviour.

Chapter 2: Finding out and exploring

Different structures can be used to assess practice and can often be a helpful way to organise your thoughts and ideas. The ORIM model is one such framework, and originates from the 'Keeping it Real' project in Sheffield focusing on raising achievement in literacy (further information can be found here: http://www.real-online.group.shef.ac.uk/). There are other examples where this framework has been used to assess and develop different areas of practice, for example, the arts.

The acronym **ORIM** stands for: **O**pportunities, **R**ecognition, **I**nteraction and **M**odelling.

You might consider the following in using this framework to assess finding out and exploring in your setting:

Opportunities – what opportunities are there for young children to find out and explore? Is there a rich variety of different experiences and activities to suit different ages and interests? Are there areas where children seem stressed/have more conflicts/appear frustrated? Why?

Recognition – What do you notice about children's explorations? Where do babies and young children seem most settled and engaged in their play? What materials or resources encourage long periods of interest or exploration?

Interaction – what sorts of interactions do you observe and notice practitioners mainly engage in? Are there different styles of interaction between different practitioners? Are there distinct ways of interacting that seem to suit particular children and different sorts of finding out and exploring?

Modelling – do practitioners model exploring materials and objects? Do you have a 'can do' attitude; do you model how to join-in with children's self-chosen play? Do you model how to find out about things by either: a) asking someone, b) looking at books or c) using the internet?

This framework might be something you could use to observe an individual child's play, one area of provision or the setting as a whole.

The right balance of child-initiated, adult-initiated and adult-led activities

How you combine adult and child-initiated activities will depend on the developmental stages of your children. For babies and toddlers, this will be guided by their personal routines and directions of play, with opportunities for one to one activities with an adult, and very small groups. Little by little, children will be ready for planned activities in small groups and a limited amount of time in larger groups.

> '*All children, throughout the EYFS, have a right to the balance of play, child-initiated and adult-led activities, indoors and outdoors, which meets their current needs and helps them to be strong and active learners*' (Moylett and Stewart 2012).

The importance of adult interactions

Chatting with children and encouraging them to share their thoughts and ideas about what they are doing helps them to make connections with their learning. Children can also be encouraged to do this together – this might be to solve a problem or develop an idea (this can be particularly beneficial as children move further into the primary curriculum – collaborating on creative projects is just one of the ways to facilitate this – see the example 'Did dragons exist?' in Chapter 5). Be alert to possibilities to facilitate learning between older and younger children.

Links to practice

- Think about why you plan an adult-led opportunity.

- What are the children going to get out of it?

- How will it add to their learning?

- What led you to plan it – i.e. does it link to something the children are interested in? Perhaps a parent has mentioned something you want to follow-up; you might wish to introduce something new/provide inspiration or you might have a specific learning intention/or area of learning you feel needs to be explored?

- How will you follow-up what you introduce or do in your adult-led time? E.g. will you add resources/books/ time to talk/observe what happens next?

Practitioners need to choose carefully how and when to interact and why. For example, you might:

- Model a particular skill or disposition (i.e. being curious, excited about finding something out)

- Teach directly how to use a specific tool (i.e. using woodwork tools)

- Hold back and 'pretend not to know something' in order to persuade a child to demonstrate their knowledge and understanding

- Encourage, coach and acknowledge a child's effort and achievement

- Comfort or offer reassurance when things don't go according to plan.

Adult modelling finding out and exploring

On the morning of my visit, children in the toddler room at Pasture's Way Nursery School were enjoying a messy play activity with corn flour and water. A few days previously, the children had enthusiastically played with corn flour in small individual bowls on the table. This had led their room leader to repeat the activity with larger quantities and in a bigger tray.

Two children were particularly enjoying watching the practitioner as she scooped up handfuls of the gloop and let if pour out of and over her fingers. They were fascinated as what appeared to be liquid changed and became solid once they touched it in the bottom of the tray. As the practitioner slowly scooped up another handful she held it over one of the children's hands, and the mixture poured through and back into the tray. 'Lovely and wet... It's cold and sticky isn't it, Sarah?'. 'Sticky' replied Sarah. The practitioner continued slowly gathering handfuls of corn-flour mixture and both children at the tray stretched their hands out to catch it as it fell. One child cupped his hands carefully, concentrating as he tipped the mixture back and forth, until most of it was gone. Sarah gathered a handful and gestured to the practitioner to hold out her hands – catching the mix as Sarah moved her hands back and forth.

The practitioner here was doing just enough to tempt the two children into the activity – she provided some appropriate language, but knew that the value of the experience lay in the physical exploration of the corn flour and water mix.

The Toddler Room Team has thought carefully about how to make best use of their space and equipment. The water tray has been used for the corn flour mix and positioned so that an adult and three children can play comfortably. The lead practitioner explained how she rotates larger pieces of equipment for malleable play and plans together with her team for children's interests. For example, several children had taken to having their short sleep after lunch in the loft space. Practitioners now tidy the loft before lunch and with the children's help, ready individual bedding and 'snuggle toys'. They have attached cotton fabric safely around the outside to create a cosy, private feel.

Supporting children's thinking

Good practitioners will support children's thinking skills when they engage in 'extra talk' – very different from just answering a question or giving an instruction. These important interactions of sustained shared thinking may involve asking an open-ended question, sharing something from your own experience, or perhaps showing your own thinking; 'I'll have to think about how to fix these wheels back on...'. Sustained shared thinking is when two or more people work together to develop an idea, sort out a problem, review an activity or extend a narrative (talking together about something) – and entails both in thinking. See **Pause for thought** on page 30 for a list of different strategies to support sustained shared thinking. It requires practitioners to

Pause for thought: Strategies for supporting sustained, shared thinking

- **Tune-in:** listen carefully to what's being said by observing body language and what the child is doing.

- **Show genuine interest:** give your whole attention to the child, maintain eye contact, acknowledge, smile and nod.

- **Respect children's own decisions and choices by inviting children to elaborate:** say things like 'I really want to know more about this' and listen and engage in the response.

- **Recapping:** 'So you think that … '

- **Offer your own experience:** 'I like to read a book if I'm on the train'.

- **Clarify ideas:** 'OK Sasha, you think if we put the snowball in the fridge, it will keep until tomorrow?'

- **Suggest:** 'You might like to try doing it this way.'

- **Remind:** 'Don't forget that you said this snowball will keep until tomorrow.'

- **Use encouragement to further thinking:** 'You have really thought hard about how to make your space rocket, where will you put the astronauts?

- **Offer an alternative viewpoint:** 'Maybe Ben 10° felt scared when he saw the monster?'

- **Speculate:** 'I wonder if the monster wanted to make friends, but could only growl?'

- **Reciprocate:** 'Thank goodness that you had your raincoat on outdoors just now Nikhil, look how wet my jumper is!'

- **Ask open questions:** 'How did you …?' 'Why does this …?' 'What happens next?' 'What do you think?'

- **Model thinking:** 'I have to think hard about how to do everything this weekend – I have to make a cake, do my shopping, visit my friend and paint my living room…'

(Acknowledgement – adapted from 'Supporting Young Children's Sustained Shared Thinking' an Exploration – Training Materials Marion Dowling.)

take a thoughtful and sensitive approach to children's play and notice what it is that they are interested in or trying to achieve.

The quality of extending child-initiated activities and interests in this way was one of the key findings of the Effective Provision of Pre-school Education research project (EPPE 1997-2003) where the most effective settings were offering the curriculum through mainly play-based activities, with an equal balance of adult/child-initiated activities.

There will also be a subtle difference between doing something for a child, and helping them to do it for themselves. It is all too easy to 'rescue' a situation if a child is struggling. A typical example is when you end-up putting children's shoes on for them most of the time (usually due to time constraints or the child's frustration), rather than staying in the moment and supporting them to do it for themselves. Both practitioner and child miss out on a potential learning

Links to practice

- Reflect on some of the suggestions to support sustained shared thinking and think about some of your own interactions with children.

- What questions or strategies do you use regularly?

- Consider recording an interaction you have with a child, and reflect on the how you support and extend the child's thinking. This can be done in pairs with another colleague to support professional development.

- Create a display with speech bubbles prompts to remind you of the different ways to support sustained shared thinking.

interaction, and this may also have implications for developing motivation and persistence (discussed further in Chapter 4).

Helping children become aware of the strategy they use that helps them to learn or get better at something is an important next step. An example of this is children using a sand-timer to make it easier to wait for turns. Or, a counting strategy – a child may find it easier to place objects in a small container and count them as they take them out one by one, rather than having them spread out in front of them. Practitioners might model their own strategy, for example writing a list.

Case study: Planning provision to support mark making

Sheringham Nursery and Children's Centre has been developing its mark-making provision in the outdoor area. They began by auditing the resources outside (using the 'Mark Making Matters' 2008 document as guidance) and the children were then observed to see where and how they were choosing to mark make.

Although some children chose to use a small outdoor table set up with paper and pencils, the majority enjoyed being on the move and mark making using other materials. For example, children were using sand, water, paint and (on one of my visits) some wonderful messy-play activities linked to an interest in potions and magic. Cauldrons full of mixtures were being stirred energetically, and children were forming marks in their 'spells' in a builder's tray. Small bottles of potion with masking-tape labels, some of which has been drawn by the children, were displayed on a shelf on the wall.

Bikes and wheeled vehicles were being used by boys and girls outdoors as part of their imaginative play, and this included some superhero and popular culture themes.

The lead practitioner discussed her findings with her colleagues and planned several important changes. First, she moved the mark making area into a larger space and added a wider variety of materials. For example: different papers, envelopes, notebooks, small tools, i.e. hole-punches, scissors, clipboards, pencils and crayons. These were organised into labelled draw units so children could access them easily. Relocating the mark making area raised its status and meant that parents were now able to see it as they arrived. Laminated superhero figures with magnetic tape were placed with whiteboard pens on the wall-mounted whiteboard nearby. A small, moveable whiteboard on wheels, colourful magnetic letters and a post-box were also added.

Pause for thought

- Children need plenty of opportunities to respond to the world and represent their experiences by finding out and exploring through mark making and drawing.

- Involving children in making books about their experiences in the setting, special outings or visitors will deepen their understanding of books and their purpose.

- Creating simple family books with photographs of family members, pets and friends will help to provide a sense of community and children's own history.

- Writing materials and books need to be placed where children will access them – often boys will prefer to mark-make outdoors and all children will be more interested to mark-make and experiment with writing when they have something to write about and it fits in with their play, e.g. shopping lists for the role-play area, telephone numbers for their favourite superheroes.

- Mark making can be encouraged in other areas, for example in the block area or in dens or tents outdoors. One setting included a small clipboard with paper and pen for children to sign, next to their adult signing-in book at reception.

The most popular resources were a selection of new, 'popular culture' writing bags. These were aimed at both boys and girls and created using lunch-bags and tool boxes and stocked with crayons, small notebooks and props. The children incorporated these immediately into their imaginative play, and carried them into all different areas of the setting.

In a large setting, the resources need to be simple, well-organised and easily replaceable. This makes it easier for children to access them, and also for other practitioners to support the lead practitioner's initiative. The next stage in this project is to continue to model and support mark-making across the setting, and involve parents. There is a well-organised toy library and following the success of the superhero writing bags, media bags are going to be developed for parents and children

Links to practice

- Take photographs of all the different examples you see of children mark-making in your setting – does this coincide with the opportunities you provide, i.e. are there places that you have planned mark making, but it just doesn't happen there? Why do you think that is?

- How might you improve opportunities for mark-making across the setting?

- Create a display to celebrate children's mark-making and emergent writing. It will be important to include examples of early mark-making – photographs of babies exploring paint marks on paper; children using paint-rollers with water; pushing fingers into sand and making patterns etc. You could:

  ○ Provide an interactive space for children to add further comments/drawings to the display.

  ○ Add 'talking-tins' or 'talking-postcards' for children to verbally record their comments.

to borrow. Rucksacks linked to a popular theme will contain a storybook, small props, a simple game and a notebook and pencils, together with a tips sheet for parents.

Some children may need your support and sensitive input to help them develop their skills as players and playful companions. To some degree a child's temperament will influence how they engage with the world but a good practitioner will tune into different possibilities to support children's explorations. In the following example, the practitioner plans a simple open-ended activity that inspires children's language and creative problem solving.

Study: Supporting bi-lingual learners

Tricia Grimes is an EAL teacher working in the EAL Peripatetic Response Team for Glasgow City Council, supporting children with English as an additional language (EAL).

I work in many culturally and socially diverse settings. Some practitioners are still developing their skills and expertise in helping children with EAL and part of my work is about supporting them to see how the simplest resource or idea can really help with inclusion and language development through the positive experience of play. It's not about fancy equipment or materials!

When children arrive in settings, some with no English language, or at the very early stages, they bring with them the richness of their home language and current communication skills. Occasionally children and families are settling-in to a very different culture to their own, but a wonderful leveller is the fact that all children, given the right circumstances will engage in play. I see my role as having three very important strands – primarily working with the children to support them to acquire language and develop their confidence and self-esteem; supporting and enabling the setting to develop their skills and confidence to continue this; and thirdly, building bridges and connections with the child's family.

When a parent arrives to see their child's early mark making (that resembles the home language script) proudly displayed, their obvious pleasure and delight highlights the importance of valuing home languages as the way forward to support the acquisition of the additional language.

Getting children outdoors and moving is essential. In one setting where the outdoor space was being developed, I set a small group of English speaking children and EAL children the challenge of moving a puddle. An important aspect of supporting those children with EAL is making sure they can enjoy play with those children already speaking English clearly – this acts as a role model and scaffolds the language. The only resource was the puddle itself, a few drops of washing-up liquid, and a long-handled broom. The activity worked on several levels:

- It was simple – all the children understood the purpose.

- It was open-ended – i.e. the children had to find some way to move the puddle. Although the activity was initiated by the adult, the children took it and made it their own.

- It had a clear goal – important for many of the boys involved – and it gave a chance for two boys to use their shared home language (one who spoke rarely was seen laughing and joining-in the play with enthusiasm).

The play offered opportunities for easy, directional language, teamwork, and most of all was fun. Some children loved using the brush to move the water, watching the bubbles grow and puff up. Others enjoyed the sensory experience of bubbly water on their hands and carrying the bubbles to the new puddle.

In addition to hearing and practicing both their home and English languages, the children were thinking deeply, supported by their interactions with each other and the practitioner.

Questions are important, but it is crucial that time is left in-between adults' questions for children to think, form their own questions, observations and comments. Tricia offered clear questions from time to time: 'How can we move it? What can we use? What works best?'. The children's responses included: 'The puddle's away now! Where has all the water gone? The puddle is getting smaller!'.

Language development is based on real experience. The learning was extended by revisiting – by drawing puddles, talking about how they moved the puddle and making a book of photographs with simple captions to describe the experience. In this way the language is recycled – the children need the opportunity to hear the same words and phrases over and over again. Photographs were also taken and displayed with both children's comments during the activity and their comments on seeing the pictures – this strengthened their language and helped to consolidate the children's thinking. It also supported practitioners to see how a simple activity could provide a rich opportunity for learning, paving the way for similar opportunities. Parents were delighted to see their children's engagement in the activity, particularly with language learning outcomes so explicitly documented.

The specialist language support teacher provided an inspiring starting point for language development, and also the opportunity for the children to engage in some deep-level thinking, as well as form friendships through their shared, positive experience.

The children are finding out and exploring, active learners and thinking creatively.

Strategies that support children to acquire a second language:

- Provide opportunities for children to hear language in meaningful contexts, again and again.

- Focus talk in the present and during experiences the child is engaged with now.

- Give children space and time and be patient – children learning a second language often go through a 'silent phase', where they understand much more than they can say.

- Plan visual clues to support children's choice and understanding of the daily routine, resources they enjoy playing with and other opportunities and activities.

Continue to talk with children with the expectation they will respond, and facilitate use of their home language.

Make sure you pronounce names correctly.

Learn a few key phrases in the child's language.

Take time to greet the child's family, make a connection and share something positive from the child's day.

Display a variety of scripts and examples of children's mark-making and drawings, as well as dual language books, home-made posters and signs.

(For further information see: Supporting children learning English as an additional language, Primary National Strategy 2007.)

Top 10 tips for finding out and exploring

1. Show your interest in discovering new things and play with children, following their ideas (without taking over) and encourage them to join-in.

2. Model finding out information through other sources, the library, by talking to another child or adult.

3. Explore music, movement and dance in open-ended ways, providing a variety of sensory materials, for example, satin ribbons and scarves.

4. Plan for visitors with particular skills – for example a brick-layer, gardener and utilise parents or friends of practitioners.

5. Notice how different children find out and discover.

6. Plan an interest table of unusual artefacts and invite parents to contribute objects or materials from home.

7. Support children's thinking through open-ended questions, comments and where appropriate, your own experience.

8. Set up a de-construction area with safe, old machinery, such as telephones, an old radio, a doorbell etc., with a selection of small tools for exploring and taking things apart.

9. Support children to manage risks and set their own challenges.

10. Create a homemade book with photographs of children finding out and exploring.

> Questions are important, but it is crucial that time is left in-between adults' questions for children to think, form their own questions, observations and comments.

Chapter 3: Playing with what they know

Playing with what they know is about children's growing ability to enter the world of make-believe and involves pretend and imaginative play. Children begin to copy and imitate the actions of close adults or older children during their first year of life, and it is from this that imaginative play begins to develop.

Imitative play involves a child recreating something in their own way from a past experience – they may imitate their parent or carer's expressions, and reenact this after the event. For example, a child will use the same gestures and comforting sounds that their mother uses with them when they fall over with a teddy.

Children bring their previous experiences to their play, and begin to experiment and represent their ideas and experiences in unique and different ways. Amy had recently moved into a new flat with her family. The bird mentioned in the painting was most likely a reflection of her favourite soft toy, 'Daffy' who could be 'very naughty' and whom Amy used to represent both herself and an imaginary friend.

Casper (p.37) represents what he knows when he pretends a plastic pot is a bird's nest, after discovering a real nest with his brother. 'My nest!' he shouts if someone tries to pick up the pot and move it.

What they know

Babies and children are playing with what they know when they:

● Pretend objects are things from their experience

● Represent experiences in their play

● Take on a role in their play

● Act-out experiences with others.

Games such as peek-a-boo promote the development of imagination because they support children to imagine what does not exist. Jack, age three, loves pretending to be a dog. His mum supports his imaginative thinking by patting him on the head, and saying 'Good boy Jack!'. On holiday, they make a small 'kennel' for him to play in, using an open umbrella on the floor, with a sheet draped across the top.

In playing with what you know children will try out different behaviour, take on diverse roles in their play and represent their experiences and imagination through the arts.

When children begin to use an object to stand for something else, for example, a wooden block for a telephone, it signals a new kind of thinking. This move from exploratory play is accompanied with an increase in language as children begin to think in abstract and creative ways. As well as language, children symbolise their thinking, feelings and ideas in other ways, for example, through:

● Mark making, drawing and writing

● Construction – block play, junk-modelling

● The arts – music, movement and dance, sculpture, painting and collage etc.

● Socio-dramatic play – creative and imaginative role-play, small world play and fantasy.

Amy, age four, spent a long time carefully painting a picture. She called it 'Building 28' and described it in the following way: "*This is a building...which I found in the night and it was empty. There are windows here... there... and these are the wings here at the side, and there is a bird. I go there at night-time. Somebody famous lives here! ... And it's me!*".

When young children first begin to pretend, the materials or objects they use will usually closely resemble the real article, such as conkers in a saucepan in the role-play area for 'cooking pasta', or a long stick with a silver dot on the end for a magic wand. Older children will be able to imagine more broadly – for example, a group of four and five year-olds build a 'bat-cave' in the woods using large branches balanced in a rough circle. They 'decorate' the cave with muddy water and leaves carried in a recycled ice-cream pot.

Imaginative experiences will encourage a wide range of skills and dispositions, such as:

Persistence, sharing, curiosity, self-discipline, concentration, respect for others, creativity, self-motivation, empathy, memory, negotiation, helpfulness, enjoyment, experimentation.

Pretend play supports children to begin to think flexibly, to consider cause and effect and 'what will happen if?'. The experience of taking on different roles supports children's self-control as they play within the limits of each role. For example, being the dog means you have to bark, eat your food from a bowl, and not sit on the bed. But if you are the dad, you can put on the kettle and tell the dog to sit! During cooperative dramatic play, children may 'step outside' the play to re-negotiate the rules or suggest a new twist to the plot.

Sometimes play can get tense and at these moments, unless a sensitive adult or more experience player steps in, the play can break down.

Emily and Samara want to play 'shoe shops' and with the help of their key person have organised the dressing-up shoes into boxes and put them out onto a low table. A squabble begins over who should measure a customer's feet. The key person intervenes "girls, I am the shoe-maker – Emily, please ask your customer what are their favourite shoe colours? And Samara, please ask your customer if they want polish for their shoes?". The key person has skilfully introduced two new possibilities that fit with the play theme and helped to extend the play. (Sharing the traditional story of *The Elves and the Shoe-maker* and a visit to a real shoe shop could also be potential next steps for learning).

Once children begin to understand that a long stick can be a magic wand, or a plastic pot can be a bird's nest, they can start to understand that marks on a piece of paper are used to represent different things.

Opportunities to **play with what you know** allow children to:

- Express their feelings and experiences

- Increase their self-confidence and sense of self

- Develop their understanding of different points of view (by taking on different roles)

- Practice story-making and develop language and vocabulary

- Represent their thoughts and ideas

- Express their culture and develop their understanding of other cultures

- Solve problems and develop skills to negotiate, join-in with other children's play and experience being in a group.

Case study: Playing with what you know

Casper found a bird's nest in the local park with his older brother, and brings it to nursery to show everyone. The children are fascinated and crowd round to look. Casper and his key person choose a safe place on a nearby shelf unit to display it. At his key person's suggestion, he helps her write a sign 'Casper's Nest – TOUCH GENTLY'.

He takes the nest home later that day. Over the next few days, as soon as Casper has arrived and hung up his coat, he immediately starts to look for a clean, empty paint pot. "This is my nest" he says. Unable to find a pot one morning, he shadows his key person until she is free from a conversation with a parent to come and help him look for one.

Each morning, he collects small, clean pieces of toilet tissue, wets them carefully and talking quietly to himself, lines the bottom of the pot with them. His key person suggests he might like to look for a toy egg to go inside the nest, and that there are some in the role-play area. Casper, delighted, finds

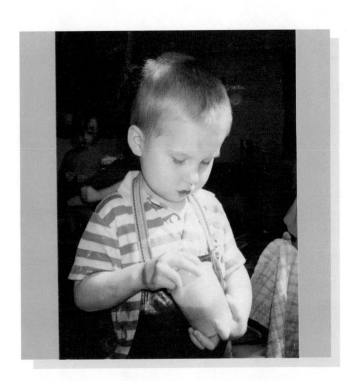

Links to practice

Casper's key person suggested they create a book about his special nest. Casper chose a piece of red card, folded it and stuck a photograph on the front of him holding his 'nest'. He shows his excellent understanding of how books work when he asks the practitioner to write on the cover 'Casper's Nest' and inside 'Once upon a time Casper made a nest and put an egg in it, The End'.

Casper was very proud of his book and took it home over the weekend to show his family. He then asked to display it on the bookshelf, so other children could see it.

- What opportunities are there for children to share special objects or experiences from home?

- How might you appropriately share these with other children in the setting?

- What possibilities are there for children to make their own, simple books or one-page posters about something they are interested in?

- How might you display these for parents and others to see?

> Small-world play provides children with the opportunity to act out feelings and events within the safe confines of play, and in some cases can provide a reflective, calm time during a busy day. Children will develop narratives and stories during small world and other role-play, and practice negotiating and listening to others.

one and pops it inside his nest, which he carries with him everywhere. He becomes distressed if anyone tries to pick it up or move it. A few days later, his key person notices that the egg has been replaced with an old electrical plug. Casper is combining his new interest with electricity with his experience of finding the bird's nest.

Casper is also demonstrating 'self-speech', as he thinks out-loud. Self-speech is for the child's benefit, and not intended for anyone else, though you may hear it. It is a strategy that helps children to think about their ideas and self-regulate their learning. Research has pointed to the positive connection between children's self-speech and problem-solving tasks.

Have you noticed if and when you talk to yourself? When do you tend to do this?

Dramatic play and socio-dramatic play

Dramatic play involves role play, puppetry, small world, a child taking on a role and fantasy play. Socio-dramatic play involves any of the above, but with the added elements of social interaction, communication and cooperation with at least one other through both action and speech. Taking on a role and acting out experiences with others gives children the chance to see things from other people's point of view. They can experiment with different ways of relating to others through the boundaries of play.

Small-world play provides children with the opportunity to act out feelings and events within the safe confines of play, and in some cases can provide a reflective, calm time during a busy day. Children will develop narratives and stories during small world and other role-play, and practice negotiating and listening to others. Adult-initiated role-play can be planned to support and develop learning from a real-life event or story text. For example, in one shared nursery and reception unit, practitioners set up the block play area to represent the story *Who Sank the Boat* (by Pamela Allen), with lengths of wood for oars, blankets for the animals and a frieze made by photocopying the pages of the book and pegging them to a washing line nearby. The learning objective was to support children's language development through their imaginative play. In addition, the children developed their:

- Personal, social and emotional skills by collaborating, developing friendships and being involved in a shared purpose.

Nathan enjoys the small-world space resources – his teacher says that he will often go and find these materials if they are not out. He is showing a particular interest in putting objects 'inside' – a pattern of play or schema.

Nathan joins in later with construction play with two other boys. He shows high levels of involvement during his solitary small world play. His teacher notes that small amounts of this one on one play seem to support Nathan to manage in small and larger groups. He is exploring different ideas through his play, and developing his fine motor skills together with his hand-eye coordination.

- What children do you know that show high levels of involvement during small-world play?

- Do some children enjoy this type of play more than others?

- What skills do you think they might be developing?

Good provision

Good provision for playing with what you know will include plenty of open-ended materials that can be used in lots of different ways. Children will benefit from a well-organised environment that takes into account the need for space and flexibility to combine different resources in creative ways:

- Good quality wooden blocks, small and hollow blocks are ideal

- Small world (people, animals, Lego blocks, cars and trains) can be combined with natural materials, such as small logs, branches, leaves or lengths of fabric

- Dolls with a range of different cultural fabrics, bedding, clothes and accessories

- Malleable materials such as play-dough, lentils, acorns etc offer children more scope for imaginative play than plastic food

- An outdoor 'mud-kitchen' with a variety of real saucepans and different tools can be created in a small corner of the outdoor area (Google 'Mud Kitchens' for further ideas)

- Dressing-up that combines favourite jobs or roles but in non-stereotypical ways (Dr's and nurses uniforms, police etc in

- Understanding the world by looking at boats, exploring and working out which block shapes worked best to build the boat.

- Mathematical understanding by directly experiencing the different size and shaped blocks; how to connect them together to make a symmetrical boat shape which was big enough to fit everyone in.

Case study: A few moments to yourself – small world play with a space rocket

The foundation stage unit at Rhodes Avenue School contains three classrooms, which open onto a central 'promenade'. Outdoors is accessed free-flow from this area. Children are busily engaged in a wide variety of activities in 'Owl' class and Nathan, sitting cross-legged by a builder's tray, has discovered that the small birthday cake 'candles' fit inside the holes on the space rocket. He concentrates carefully as he places a small 'candle' in each of the holes, and although two other children are playing nearby, he remains focused on what he is doing. Picking up one of the astronauts, he places the figure inside the rocket, closes the door and slowly lifts the rocket up, as if it is launching into space. One of the sticks falls out, and he brings the rocket back down into the tray. Collecting the sticks, he begins to add them carefully to the boot of one of the space vehicles.

The block-play area at Pasture's Way Nursery is well organised with a good selection of large hollow blocks, small unit blocks, tiny coloured blocks and an interesting variety of small world resources, vehicles, planes, lengths of fabric and different books, both fiction and non-fiction to support play. The floor is carpeted to soften noise and provide a comfortable space for everyone to be at floor level. Practitioners have thought carefully about keeping the space clear of anything that is not really necessary.

Currently there is a notice board with photographs and observations linked to children's ongoing schema – patterns of play, templates on shelves for easy tidying-up, and one corner of the room is sectioned off, allowing for quieter, more intimate small world, looking at books and talk. Adjacent to this, a small round table with pencils and paper has proved popular, and is placed in such a way that an adult can sit one to one with a child, but also observe and keep an eye on what's going on in the rest of the room.

On the day I visited, the room was a hive of activity – noisy, focused play was in full flow, with at least five different play scenarios happening simultaneously.

Children were playing individually, in pairs, and in the example below, a piece of play that one child initiated developed into a whole group's exploration of small planks being used as 'skateboards'.

Simon (4.5 years) entered the room and spent a few moments watching. He then walked over to where the small planks were piled together and began searching through them. "You look like you're looking for something particular" I commented. "Yes, he replied, my skateboard". "Ahhh" I said (this can be a useful response, when you want to convey interest, but not interrupt the flow). He found his 'skateboard' – a small plank with writing and marks on one side. Tucking it under his arm, he repositioned a long hollow block in the centre of the room, adding a triangular block at the end to form a slope. Then, carefully balancing on the plank on top of the block, he pushed off, slid down the slope, spreading his arms wide in imitation of a real skate-boarder. He quickly returned for another go, experimenting with different positions, and every time he achieved his goal of remaining upright, he grinned at the practitioner nearby. Soon, two other boys joined in, attracted by his enthusiasm.

simple tabards work well). Include clothes that are easy for children to put on, with lengths of fabric, scarves and shoes, interesting textured fabrics and tunics representing a variety of cultural backgrounds.

- Collections of different materials can be rotated and will help you respond to different interests or ideas in the moment. For example:

  ○ A variety of chunky, glass perfume bottles

  ○ Shells and pebbles, small round metal scouring sponges

  ○ Jewellery – necklaces, bracelets, flower clips and collars

  ○ Paper straws, pipe-cleaners

  ○ Hats and sunglasses

  ○ Wigs

  ○ A picnic basket

  ○ First-aid kits with home-made bandages

  ○ Animal masks

  ○ Small pets, pet baskets and bedding.

At one point he needed to be reminded to keep the plank below head height – he'd discovered he could slide it between the bars of the loft area. The practitioner encouraged him to demonstrate how he positioned his feet and used his arms to balance to the other children who were keen to have a go. Several girls who had been playing a game of 'police' nearby joined in, but the triangular block kept sliding away: "I wonder what would happen if you turned that one over?" asked the practitioner. Simon and his friend moved the block, and discovered that this worked. Six children were now fully engaged in the skateboard play.

This example demonstrates the three characteristics of effective learning in action. Children are learning through the three prime areas of development – physical, personal, social and emotional and communication and language. They are also exploring some aspects of expressive arts and design, mathematics and understanding the world.

A commentary on the characteristic of playing and exploring could include any of the following statements: 'Simon has a particular interest in skateboards, and engages in open-ended play. He is able to pretend an object (the small plank) is something from his experience. He shares his knowledge with others, demonstrating how to balance and slide carefully. He initiated this activity and set his own challenge, confident to have a go, and was able to come up with his own idea to improve the slope'.

together with the children may give you some insight into the different themes children are exploring, and encourage them to come up with ideas to extend their own play and learning. (See the idea for 3D Planning on pages 26 and 27 Chapter 2 and the practice example Hindley's pre-school.)

A stage area can offer children different opportunities for performance, movement and dance and can be combined with musical resources, a CD player, chiffon scarves and home-made books with children's favourite rhymes, poems and songs.

Children will benefit from uninterrupted time to immerse themselves in imaginative play, as well as adult support at different points.

Practice example – acting out experiences with others in the home setting

Nikki Cox plans a variety of materials and props for imaginative play in her childminding practice.

I do provide some 'real' things, for example small cups, plates and dressing-up clothes in a home-corner space in my front room, but I like to balance this with open-ended resources, for instance – lengths of fabric, cushions and den-making materials. Two of my boys have really enjoyed playing with

Superheroes

Lengths of fabric (in colours that link to favourite characters) and pipe-lagging (grey foam tubing available from builder's merchants) will help children create their own superhero capes, swords or light sabres. Shop-bought superhero costumes tend to be difficult for young children to get on and off independently, and limit children's creativity and imagination in devising their own accessories and plot lines.

One of the challenges of superhero-themed play can be encouraging it to develop more imaginatively from repetitive, physical play. Holland (2003) recommends taking time to understand and not assume a popular culture interest, until you know what the game is about. This will help you to plan appropriately to support and extend the play. Different combinations of role-play may develop superhero play. For example a superhero den or headquarters; a hospital for injured heroes; a secret potions cave (McTavish, 2008). Planning

these recently – they both get different things from the play. One gets real pleasure from the social aspect, doing things together with his friend, whilst the other relishes the opportunity to design, build and make dens. I encourage them to make their own decisions about what they need.

Nikki described a recent interaction: "This fleece is not big enough! What could you do?". The boys took the covers off the sofa, but found it difficult to join the two fabrics together: "What do you think would help?", "pegs!" they shouted, so we went shopping to buy pegs. I like to let them expand their play, so I am quite happy for them to start in the living room, spread into the hall and end up by the kitchen cupboards!

I don't feel I need to be involved in the play all the time – though I do join-in if they invite me. I feel if I'm too involved, then they don't get the chance to make their own suggestions and the play doesn't really get going. I learn a lot just listening – this helps me to plan next steps for each of them.

I take advantage of local events and special activities – we recently went to hear a storyteller at the local library who told stories about space travel and the moon. The children made rockets out of recycled materials and were pleased to be able to bring them home. They enjoyed this outing, so the next day I planned some new role play resources, to see how they might develop their ideas. I organised four small chairs with rubber quoits on the seats for 'steering wheels', silky fabric and crinkly, silver 'athlete blankets' and some cushions. I put on my bubble machine, which gave it a really magical feel. The children spent a long time playing creatively. They built their own rocket, did count downs and lift-off scenarios and developed some very imaginative stories. This was one of them; they were both going through the clouds, and then landed on a planet: "Not our planet...".

"Can you remember the planet we live on?" I asked. "We live on Earth!" they shouted. The older of the boys said: "Let's call it Bubble Planet!" where upon they both jumped up and started chasing the bubbles, popping them, and trying to catch them in a heart-shaped wooden box: "Let's catch them, and we can take them back on our rocket".

Communication and Language

- In the example above an older child scaffolds play and language for a younger child.

Pause for thought

- Taking children to special performances or outings can inspire new learning and give everyone a breath of fresh air.

- What possibilities are there to go to local events to hear a storyteller, see a play for young children or experience a soft-play facility?

- How could you involve parents in the trip?

- How might you follow-up and deepen the children's experience back in your setting?

- Nikki does not give the boys all the answers, instead she asks open questions and leaves time for them to think and come up with their own ideas.

- Consider why you involve yourself in an imaginative play scenario – what are the children gaining from your involvement?

- Consider recording your interaction during an imaginative play opportunity, and review how you support the communication and language taking place. It might support you to do this as a shared professional development exercise with a colleague you feel comfortable with.

Playing in a group

'Becoming a player' – the ability to participate in group play involves developing a variety of different skills. Children need to learn particular strategies to enter a group without being rejected. They need to be flexible and creative in order to join-in with different play themes and scenarios.

Children need to develop skills in the following areas:

1. Be able to join a group

2. Be approving and supportive of their peers

3. Be able to manage conflicts appropriately

4. Exercise sensitivity and tact.

(Rubin, 1983 in Bruce, p.191, 3rd Ed, 2005.)

A skilful practitioner will know that sometimes they need to become an imaginative play coach and mentor, to support children to develop these skills. Modelling for children how to join-in will help show them different ways they can begin to do this for themselves.

Playing simple games with rules will help children to regulate themselves and practice turn-taking in a framework that makes sense to them. At Pasture's Way Nursery School, a group of boys regularly began to initiate a game of football, but needed help from a practitioner to keep the game going and to each take turns to try and score a goal and be in goal. She introduced the idea of a 'score-board', bringing a small whiteboard outdoors near the pitch for them to scribe the number of turns and goals they scored. She developed this further by providing numbered tabards, so they could plan what order they would take their turns. Once they had played this several times with the practitioner modelling how to play 'with football rules' they were able to regulate it for themselves. This supported their self-confidence and skills to work together as a team – a football team!

Imaginative play for older children

Children develop important social and cognitive skills through playing with what they know. They will be developing self-regulation, and amongst many other things, their communication and language will be enhanced. In her fascinating research Pat Broadhead (Ch.3, 2010) describes the impact of a new area of play provision – the 'whatever you want it to be place' for ages from three to six years (nursery through to year 1), and the deep thinking that emerged.

The 'whatever you want it to be place' was set up where there was room – in one case, it was organised outdoors, and relocated to a wide corridor space during winter.

The 'whatever you want it to be place' is open-ended (unlike a traditional 'home-like' role-play space) in order to allow the children to determine their play themes and use resources to support their activities through social interaction. The researchers found that the older children often needed time to rediscover their ability to play creatively and imaginatively. Given time to develop, children incorporated their new skills of reading and writing into their play.

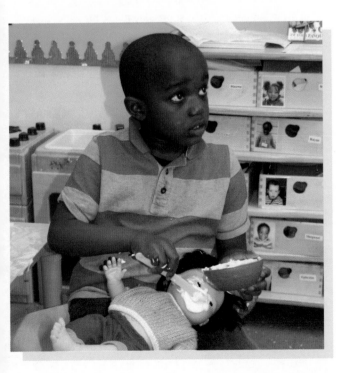

Links to practice

- If you were to set up a 'whatever you want it to be place' (and of course, the children can decide the name of their 'place' – one group in the study called it the 'magic space') where would you site it and what resources would you provide to promote open-ended play?

- Here are some suggestions – clothes horses, lengths of fabric, scarves, clothes pegs, cardboard boxes of different shapes and sizes.

- Tell the children that this is their space to play ... whatever they like (obviously, your usual rules of respectful, caring and appropriate behaviour will apply) and see what happens.

- Observe the play and discuss with colleagues what aspects of playing and exploring are involved to see?

Cultural perspectives

Although adults will often delight in children's enjoyment of play, they may not approve of all forms of play (Brooker, p.30, 2010) and in some cases, there may be different value placed on certain types. Imitative play that is seen to develop life-skills – cooking, putting dolls to bed, clearing up the house, talking on the telephone and going shopping etc. may be viewed as more beneficial than highly imaginative, fantasy play. Some play experiences may be relegated to 'after you have done your work'– practicing letters, sounds and reading. It will be helpful if practitioners are sensitive to the cultural origins of these values, and take the time to talk and share learning with parents.

In some cases, sensitive thought needs to be given to 'forming a bridge' between one cultural viewpoint and another. For example, a father bringing his young daughter to nursery was upset when he saw what he viewed as 'baby play-stuff' – play dough with rolling pins and wooden knifes – and told her to go and play with different things where she would learn something 'about letters'. The practitioner realised a better move might have been to add plastic letter cutters to support the girl's enjoyment of play dough and have a conversation with the father to help make the link between play, literacy and learning at school.

Case study: Orange Soup – time to settle-in before imaginative play

Earlier that morning at Pastures Way Nursery School, a small group of children had taken part in a short, adult-led story group. This group was facilitated very creatively by a practitioner who used a 'story basket' to support talk and possibilities for further play and learning. Maya had arrived as the group began and seemed a little tired, taking time to settle-in. She enjoyed a warm cuddle with the practitioner at the end of the group, who acknowledged how difficult it was to join-in when you had only just arrived. Maya happily went off to play, her energy restored.

The practitioner told me that she had decided to use her story basket to respond to the children's interest in fire. This had been prompted by both the timing of the Olympic torch travelling close by the setting and a visit from the local fire brigade. She showed me some of the children's 'fire pictures'

Pause for thought

When twins Justin and Jemima joined their local nursery, the practitioners were quick to find out that Dad (who usually dropped off and picked up the children) played drums. He was invited to come in and run a drumming session with the children. The twins were thrilled to have their dad in the setting, especially Jemima who could be quite shy. Children and practitioners enjoyed the experience, and photographs from the drumming day were displayed.

When they moved into primary one, Dad was surprised and pleased when he arrived at sports day to see his national flag of Trinidad and Tobago flying alongside others.

- Are different experiences represented in small-world materials? For example, not all children live in a large house – a series of flats can be created by sticking small, strong cardboard boxes together – do this with the children so they are part of the design process.

- Do you plan for children to represent their feelings and recent experiences by making sure there are appropriate resources, for example, dolls with miniature nappies, talcum powder etc. for the arrival of a new baby?

- Could a new imaginative space be created, away from your regular role play/home-corner? This might be a 'whatever you want it to be place' or a small garden shed, a 'grass' umbrella to form an alternative roof etc.

Links to practice

- Consider children and families that access your setting – how do you reflect different communities in your role play and other provision?

- Are you aware if some types of play are valued more than others?

- What opportunities do you provide to welcome culturally-rich experiences into the setting?

– several drawing and collage artworks that the children had created to represent their experiences of fire.

During the story-basket session, she introduced a variety of interesting props – which included: a fire fighter's outfit with hat and gloves; a breathing mask; a foam water-spray pump (for the fire-hose); a small silver desk bell (very popular); a pair of blue wellingtons; a cardboard/tissue-paper Olympic torch; several books about fire-fighting and a small poster. A new parent who had stayed to settle her child was delighted when he tried on the fire-fighter's costume and spoke a few words in English to the practitioner. The children were encouraged by the practitioner to explore the props, try things out and ask questions. One boy was thrilled to hold the cardboard torch, lifting it high above his head, in imitation of a real torch-bearer. The bell prompted talk about when you would use a bell, and what sort of bells the fire station would have, and one child recognise it might 'go in a hotel'.

Later the same morning I saw Maya sitting comfortably on a large hessian cloth, playing alongside another child, surrounded by a rich variety of heuristic play materials. These included: colourful, dried slices of orange, seed pods, small sections of wood, wooden curtain rings and fir cones. Maya told me she was cooking, and she showed me a carefully constructed 'fire' with sections of small logs, orange slices and seed pods: "I'm making orange soup. It's going to be yummy-yummy, in your tummy! ... This is a splendid fire!" she announced. "I will show my mummy and daddy… And when they come, they're gonna say 'It's a splendid fire!'".

Communication and language

- The creative idea of the story-basket supported talk and conversation between the children.

- The parent visitor, whose first language was not English, enjoyed watching her child play, soaking up the friendly atmosphere of the practitioner's 'story'.

- Children were able to go at their own pace, and the creative use of props provided ways to scaffold and prompt language.

Inspiring new learning

Observing children's interests and planning how to extend learning will be part of your role as a good practitioner. One of the ways you can do this is to recognise how a child represents their experiences through playing and

Pause for thought

Maya is deeply involved in this activity she has chosen for herself, and the heuristic play resources are being well used. The other child playing alongside has set himself the challenge of building a tower with thin slices of wood. He needs encouragement to build the tower again when it accidently falls over. Maya joins the practitioner in encouraging him, and passes him several pieces of wood the right size. This spurs him on, and he completes his tower (a younger child learning from an older child). The open-ended materials provide the opportunity for 'instinctive maths' (Moyles, p.196, 2010) and they are being used here creatively for symbolic play. Maya has developed a story – she describes her fire to the adults, but also speaks to herself quietly as she continues to build it. The open-ended possibilities of the play materials allow her to explore her experience from the morning group session.

Pumpkin Soup (Helen Cooper, Corgi, 1999) would be a good book to read, and for the Forest school practitioners in the setting to plan a real fire experience.

exploring and offer them a new and novel way to repeat this. Understanding children's patterns of play – schema theory, can help you to put this into practice.

Your observations of a child's schema will be a useful addition to a commentary on the characteristics of effective learning. It may also include suggestions of how parents might provide appropriate play at home to support both schemas and the characteristics of effective learning. You will find an example commentary below linked to the practice example.

Practice example – representing experiences through schematic play

At Pastures Way Nursery School, practitioners have attended an in-service training on schemas, and are alert to noticing these in children's play. Several practitioners have observed an interest in connecting (joining or fastening things together, sometimes taking things apart). Children have been wrapping and winding

Example commentary

Characteristics of effective learning

Theo shows particular interests and is enthusiastic about participating in open-ended play. He has a positive, 'can do' attitude.

He is able to concentrate and pay attention to detail. He confidently tries again if something doesn't work first time and celebrates his success with adults and other children. He takes time to solve problems and creatively tries out different ideas.

His enjoyment and focus in the 'tape and poles' activity (attach a photograph for parents to see this in action) suggests he may be exploring a connecting schema. A connecting schema is a fascination of joining, connecting or taking things apart.

He may like to play with string, masking tape, construction kits or build a railway at home. Books like *The very busy Spider* by Eric Carl, or perhaps *Oy! Get off my Train* by John Burningham will support his learning, and I'm sure he will be interested in chatting about how things connect and join together.

lolly sticks with wool or string and joining paper straws, pipe cleaners and bottle tops with tape and paper (also shows core and radial patterns).

Practitioners discussed their observations and the team-leader planned an inspiring activity outside to provide children with the chance to connect large-scale using bamboo sticks and a variety of colourful sticky-tape. The practitioner involved the children right from the start, by inviting them to help decide where the bamboo poles should go – did they have enough? Initially, she imagined that the children would only wind the tape around individual poles, and she helped to begin the play by directly teaching how to attach the tape and wind quickly to secure it. Once children had mastered this, they discovered that the tape could be stretched out...very long! Two children worked together to stretch their tape across the play area, delighted to see how long they could make it go.

One child had the idea to join his tape to another stick, and then another and this prompted some excited and energetic connecting by an enthusiastic group of (mainly) boys for the whole morning. They even included a folding clothes horse in this connecting activity. The practitioner supported the play by describing what she saw, using key words to match the children's actions and took photographs along the way. She helped the children negotiate turns and reflected back their imaginative ideas – some children were focused on the physical aspect of connecting and joining, but some described their imaginative ideas of making a trap or designing a castle.

One child with a specific special need was welcomed into the play, and spent time carefully making his way over or under – with encouragement from other children if he became stuck or caught.

The practitioner protected the play by setting a clear limit about the bikes (drawing a large piece of tarpaulin across to prevent bikes coming too close) and negotiating for 'tomorrow' when one child arrived with a pair of scissors!

Case study: Secret treasure – Socio-dramatic play with other children and an adult

In the outdoor area at Rainbow Nursery the sandpit is surrounded on all sides by wooden decking, allowing sand to be transported to and fro easily. If they wish, children can access water from a nearby water barrel and carry it in small watering cans. Buckets are provided in an old plastic rubbish bin next to the sandpit. On the morning of my visit, a selection of spades had been placed standing upright in the sand, looking rather like leaning soldiers, waiting to be given their orders!

When I arrived in the garden a little later that morning, two boys and their practitioner were deeply engrossed in exploring a tunnel that one of the boys had created. The practitioner was listening carefully to the boy's comments: "I'm blocking it up, where the treasure came from, so no-one can get it … shall we wash it?" holding the treasure carefully in his hand he runs over to wash it under the water butt tap and returns full of purpose: "shall we cover it up? … I made a little gap… it's a secret, so no one knows… It's secret treasure!".

Tyler hides his treasure again at the bottom of the tunnel. The narrative continued…

"This is where the trains go… (pointing to the tunnel in the sand). Children have to make the hole. But no trains can make holes. They're not allowed… that's what this is for" (and points to a small toy barrier gate, which he has placed at one end of the tunnel to stop the train getting through).

The practitioner says: "I have found a little white ball..?"

"No, that's treasure…"

She says that all this talk of treasure reminds her of some small treasure boxes they have inside – does he remember, they played with them last week…and asks if he would like one with some more treasure.

Tyler is delighted when she returns, and carefully places the small white ball inside the treasure box. "I'm shutting the treasure box" and then says: "I need this treasure at home", whereupon he and the practitioner have a lively interchange about whether or not all the treasure can go home, with the practitioner making a clear boundary that he can choose one piece of treasure to take home if he likes. Tyler experiments with putting sand inside the box, rinses it off under the water and takes his treasure over to show another practitioner.

He returns to the sandpit just as tidy-up time begins and with great gusto digs a hole with the help of another boy and buries his treasure box. A few minutes later several children approach, intrigued by this new mound in the sandpit. Tyler is clearly anxious that his treasure is going to be dug up. As I am close by with notepad and a pen, I ask Tyler if he would like to put a sign on his buried treasure. His face brightens and

he asks me to write 'don't dig this up, it's for pirates, signed Tyler'. He rushes inside and returns with a piece of sellotape to stick the note to the sand! Although of course this does not work, he is undeterred, and confidently buries one corner of the note firmly under some sand, leaving the writing showing. He pats the sand down, and runs off to fetch the practitioner to show her.

The team at Rainbow Nursery put a great deal of time and effort into organising an inspiring place to play and explore. They plan for a long morning, with a 'help-yourself' tray of snacks supplied by a parent on a rota system. This allows children to have a long uninterrupted time to play with practitioners on hand to support and extend the learning.

Planning for next steps – following children's interests

At the end of each session practitioners at Rainbow Nursery have a brief discussion about what they have observed and noticed about children's play and exploration. Practitioners in this setting use an A4 **PLOD** (possible lines of development) planning sheet to note children's interests and plan potential next steps for learning. These next steps are then added to the weekly plan, which is not overfull: "we do this so we can include spontaneous interests or events that happen during

Pause for thought

- The richness of the play in the example above is due to a number of factors. The provision is deceptively simple – there is plenty of space to play, with resources arranged in tempting ways for children to access them independently. In several of my observations at Rainbow Nursery, practitioners offered other resources to extend the play, and knew exactly where to find them.

- None of the practitioners were writing notes – all were involved in children's play or in conversations with parents who were settling children in at the start of term.

- Do you feel you know where to find things in your setting? Do the children?

Top 10 tips for playing with what they know

1. Model pretending that an object is something else (a cup becomes a hair-dryer).

2. Model 'playing a role' and join-in sometimes with children's imaginative play.

3. Plan a visit (or invite visitors to your setting) with a person in a particular role in the community, for example the local 'lollypop' person, the vet or the fire station.

4. Introduce children to something new through a visit to see dance or music.

5. Be alert and sensitive to a child who is attempting to join a group. Do not immediately jump in to help; are they able to manage on their own?

6. Allow children to combine and transport different resources to suit their play.

7. Plan opportunities where possible where an older child can demonstrate a skill or role to a younger child.

8. Introduce different voices or characteristics to simple rhymes or songs, for example be a grumpy giant singing 'Twinkle little star'.

9. Share good quality story books.

10. Provide a range of non-fiction books about different jobs and experiences from around the world.

the week". This allows them to go with the flow of children's learning. Different activities and experiences are colour-coded to show a clear link to areas of learning and development. Individual observations are added to children's portfolios alongside photographs and examples of work, and in addition, group learning experiences initiated by the children are celebrated in their 'Group Learning Book'.

In order to support children playing with what they know practitioners need to:

- Be emotionally present and available

- Have a well-organised storage system of resources and materials, and know where to find things swiftly

- Think creatively about how best to extend a child's play, or offer something new to scaffold the child's learning.

They will be working within Vygotsky's theory – the 'zone of proximal development' which describes the gap between what a child can do alone and what they can do with the help of someone more skilled or experienced, who can be an adult or another child (Pound, p.40, 2005). Vygotsky emphasised the social context of learning, recognising the importance of families, communities and other children. He saw children's actions with each other

as important – an older child who helps a younger child gains as much from the experience, for in helping, they clarify what they already know. This is where the familiar term 'scaffolding' originates, and is precisely what the practitioner did when she followed Tyler's lead 'pretending' to find some treasure herself. She continued to scaffold his learning, by waiting and listening and then made a decision to offer him a small treasure box with 'more treasure', which made a connection with a previous experience.

Chapter 4: Being willing to 'have a go'

Playing and exploring

Finding out and exploring

Playing with what they know

Being willing to 'have a go'

Children who are encouraged to experiment, try new things, ask questions and understand that they have an effect on people and their surroundings will be willing to 'have a go'.

When adults support a child's innate urge to explore and provide a rich and interesting environment, they are sowing the seeds for a confident child who will actively seek out new experiences. This emotional security will stand children in good stead, as they adventure into the world, finding out, taking risks and learning through trial and error.

Chapter 4: Being willing to 'have a go'

Not all children will be full of confidence to 'have a go'. Sometimes this may just be part of their natural make-up, but it may also be part of a deeper issue, where a child has already learnt that what they do does not matter, and they give up trying. Babies will take their emotional cues from the adults and children around them, a warm smile and nod of encouragement will communicate 'It's alright to explore'. But if adults are anxious, or try to control too much, children quickly pick up on this and act accordingly.

Babies and children are willing to 'have a go' when they:

● Initiate activities

● Seek new experiences and challenges

● Show a 'can do' attitude

● Take a risk, engage in new experiences and learn from failures

Those children who struggle and avoid new encounters will need sensitive adult support, building on familiar routines and taking advantage of 'just enough' new experiences.

Adults will do a great deal to support a child's willingness to have a go, by showing their own 'can do' approach to life. The dispositions we want to encourage, we need to be willing to demonstrate ourselves.

This aspect of playing and exploring particularly links to the characteristic active learning – and supporting children's motivation. Children who can stay focused for a period of time; persist even though something is difficult and delight in their achievements will develop confidence in their own learning.

Study: Having a go with the basket

Toby, seven-months-old, is sitting on a blanket outside on the grass. A round, shallow basket with a selection of plastic bottles filled with different objects and tied with colourful ribbons has been placed next to him. Toby has enjoyed these shaker bottles before, but today he tips all the bottles out and grasps the basket in both hands. Leaning forward, legs spread, toes curled, he tries to lift the basket up. He manages to raise it to his chest but then overbalances and falls backwards, with the basket rolling sideways. His mum calmly puts a hand under his back, popping him back up, reassuring him 'there you go, you're alright… here's your basket back'.

Toby is willing to have another go and leans further forward this time. He grasps the basket again and lifts … and wobbles as he brings it up to his chest, and drops it. "You lifting the basket Toby?" encourages his mum. Toby rolls the basket around until it is upside down, and then lifts it again, moving it up over his face, where he is hidden from view for a few minutes. With a last big effort, he lifts the basket above his head. Toby is clearly delighted with this achievement and smiles broadly at us both. (We both clap!)

Communication and language

In the example above, Toby's mum gives a series of positive emotional cues:

● She is relaxed and smiles as he plays

● She stays calm when he topples over and pops him back up

● She lets him know it's alright to explore the basket by smiling and says "here's your basket back…"

● She claps when he shows his delight in his achievement.

How do you show children it is alright to 'have a go' through your body language, gestures and verbal encouragement?

Planned, purposeful play means you will be planning

Links to practice

● What children do you know who show a 'can do' attitude, the confidence to find out and try again even if they don't succeed first time round?

● What sorts of activities and experiences do these children enjoy?

● Are there other children who perhaps are less confident, hang back, need more time and your encouragement to try something new?

● What sorts of activities and experiences do these children enjoy?

to do, and not giving enough, when there is the risk that they might give up. Succeeding in something you have set out to do is immensely valuable for children's self-esteem and self-efficacy (believing you can do it). The theme tune of 'Bob the Builder' comes to mind: 'We can do it, yes we can!' and in my experience has sometimes proved a useful motivator to support a child to continue having a go.

The dispositions of motivation and persistence develop when children are able to practice dealing with difficulties and experience some frustration. This will support their developing problem-solving abilities.

Children get a sense of achievement by taking part in real activities and seeing a process through from beginning to end. They also learn that things can take time, and particular steps have to be followed in the right sequence. Cooking and gardening activities demonstrate this. They are learning by taking reasonable risks and through making mistakes. A good practitioner will help children reflect on the positive side of making mistakes, and how much we can learn from them.

Older children can be encouraged to review their learning with adult support. For example, you might set two children the task of finding 'something out about the sand and water they are mixing together'. You might ask them to report back two things they really enjoy and two things that are difficult. Some reception and Key Stage 1 teachers plan a review time to support this process. This also builds children's confidence to share some of their learning.

Case study: Willing to 'have a go' – in the dark

The practitioner in the rising threes room at Pastures Way Nursery School has planned an exciting new opportunity to 'play in the dark'. A set of new torches has arrived and the children are very interested in them. The practitioner told me that one of her learning intentions was to support the children's self-confidence and give them an opportunity to try something really different.

Making good use of a room that is free for part of the morning, she has set up a series of dens. These include a small tepee tent, which is shared across the setting, a wooden cube that has been borrowed from the block area and several cardboard boxes. The floor is covered with a soft rug. The children have been told they are going to be exploring in the dark and have

opportunities for children to initiate play to support their learning, together with adult-initiated and small, adult-led groups. Children's interests and passions will spark when they are enabled to seek their own experiences – your job will be to keep these sparks firing through your plans for enhanced provision, adult-initiated and adult-led groups.

Carr (2004) describes the process of growing and developing positive dispositions in three stages – being ready, being willing and being able. This means that successful learners are willing to have a go, recognise when and how to use their skills and why. Carr and Claxton (2004) also highlight the importance of the learning community to support and grow positive dispositions. They explain these environments as ranging from prohibiting, affording, inviting and potentiating – with the potentiating learning environment being the most powerful. This describes a learning environment where positive learning dispositions are not only encouraged, but are stretched to grow.

In the case study on page 54, a potentiating learning environment has been developed over time to support nursery and reception age children who are learning from each other.

The right amount of adult support

There is a fine balance between giving a child just enough help and support to succeed in something they have chosen

their torches with them. When I come into the room, the children have just arrived and are very quiet.

This small room has no direct sunlight, although some light filters in through two doors, and we can see other children going about their day in another room.

The practitioner sits close by her small group, who have begun to experiment by shining their torches at the dens, up at the ceiling and at each other's faces. The practitioner reminds them to point the light away from their friends' eyes.

Slowly, the children begin to talk and venture towards the tepee – "It's dark" says one child in a hushed voice.

Gradually, with a little encouragement, several children go inside the tent.

One of them says: "This is my house" and they begin a game of going in and out and 'visiting', saying hello to each other through the tent's window. One child is fascinated by the torchlight inside the tepee and traces the shape with his hand as it moves.

The practitioner makes sure that everyone is comfortable, and keeps her comments to a minimum, reflecting back what she hears and every so often giving a little encouragement.

The child who was first to go inside the tepee now finds the wooden cube and crawls in, shouting out to the others to visit, and they all need some help not to get too squashed!

There is a pleasurable feeling in the room that the exploring has really begun, as the children's voices get louder and they begin to move around the room more. A few moments later the children have all found their 'own house', and go back and forth visiting each other.

There is a slight mishap when one child tips out of a box; and one child screams with excitement, but the practitioner calmly reassures this child by placing a hand on his back and saying "remember, we are being quiet in this room".

At one point one of the children says: "Let's make a bed" – a piece of fabric is provided. As I'm sitting nearby I am instructed to 'pat it out' and first one child and then the whole group lie down in the bed. Another piece of fabric is provided for a blanket and the child who initiated the bed-making begins to 'snore'. "Is that someone snoring?" asks the practitioner in a pretend surprised voice, amidst the children's delighted giggles.

Case study – Maths provision

At New River Green Children's centre, the setting has been developing its mathematical provision.

This has included the following initiatives:

- Organising and adding new labels to all the mathematical resources.

- Supporting children who are interested in numbers and counting to explore the environment and devise their own number line, linked to children's observations.

- Children have been really encouraged to have a go, and as a result have developed their confidence and knowledge around mathematical language and thinking. This has been enriched through regular songs, fun rhymes and counting games.

- Creating a parent's notice board, where each week a different parent is invited to scribe the written names for numbers in their home language. This display is full of wonderful photographs of mathematical investigating across the setting.

- Practitioners, children and parents have increased their confidence to 'have a go' at mathematical problems. The children have created a simple counting resource by decorating a box with numbers on each side, with a corresponding number of old-fashioned clothes pegs.

Several children then practice their snoring and one of them taps the floor – "it's me tapping my feet" she says. A conversation takes place about 'all the noisy sleepers' and then one child makes a connection to a favourite story and says Plod, plod, plod and creates a new line 'snore, snore, snore'.

The importance of risk and challenge

A new statement from the health and safety executive was published in 2012, to highlight concerns that a too-sterile play environment was preventing children from learning through appropriate challenges, and could result in children not having the chance to 'expand their learning and stretch their abilities'.

Careful thought and consideration needs to be given to keeping young children safe, but this must be balanced with supporting the development of important life skills. Confidence and self-esteem grows through learning how to manage new experiences, thus children will be motivated and willing to try again.

Reviewing your accident book to see where accidents really do happen will help you to think how to prevent these in future.

Links to practice

- Avoid saying "be careful … you might fall!" as invariably a child will. Instead, promote responsibility – "what do you need to do to stay safe?" or "well done, I like how you took your time to climb the steps carefully".

- Plan appropriate physical challenges to allow children to test a range of physical skills, particularly in the outdoor environment.

- Consider how you might facilitate safe rough and tumble play – children are learning important limits during this type of physical play. Several gym mats, or a rug with cushions around will be one way to do this.

- Rather than telling children they are clever … praise and acknowledge their efforts: "I like how you held onto the bars to help you swing across".

- Model how to ask for help and encourage children to think about what help they might need.

Case study – A learning environment

At College Green Nursery School the reception and nursery age children share an interesting and creative environment. Practitioners have responsibility for planning and resourcing a specific curriculum area. Brief team discussions at the end of each session help practitioners decide what changes to make to the provision to extend children's learning and what new provocations might be appropriate for the next day.

The reception teacher noted the variety of learning styles in her group: 'children are showing lots of diverse interests. Some are flitting back and forth between different things, some children are revisiting interests they have explored already and some are very firmly connected to a particular fascination.'

Two children (one nursery age, one reception) developed an interest in rockets and outer space. The practitioner set up a small world role play with rocks, moon-dust, figures and other props which prompted lots of shared imaginative play and questions about planets. She suggested they find out more by looking at a book ... which they did and then one of the children said: "Let's look on the internet for information about planets". Nina, the reception age child, wrote 'planets' in the search engine...

The following is the practitioner's commentary:

We all looked at the planet Mars carefully and described what we saw. Samir, you said: "It's all brown maybe there's brown rocks and it looks hot!". Well Samir you were right once again because I also read that Mars was filled with rocks and dust. I carried on reading and there was another bit of information I didn't know about Mars! It has the biggest volcano ever!! Nina you then said: "Volcanoes have lots of red liquid – It explodes up like this! And you showed me with you hands how big the explosion would be. "It's so big" you continued... "It's GIGANTIC!". So after the astronauts had gathered all of their information we decided that we had to report back to your fellow astronauts and make an information page about Mars. So Samir you went to another computer and opened the 2Simple program because you wanted to paint a picture of Mars to show your astronaut friends what it looked like...

The children, now firmly in the role of astronauts, created information sheets about the planet Mars and sent this back to Earth. Nina used her knowledge of letters and sounds to write her own report: 'Mars has a gigantic volcano and dust.' and uses

a full-stop in the right place. The children also discussed with their practitioner how to stay safe on the internet and together came up with ideas for next steps for learning, including the possibility of creating a small book about 'planets' so other children in the setting could learn about them too!

The practitioner here is demonstrating her own disposition to be willing to 'have a go', and her enthusiasm for finding out about planets is infectious.

She facilitates a short fifteen-minute group each day with a focus on new sounds and high-frequency words. This is followed up across the setting in different areas. For example: "We hide objects beginning with our focus sounds in envelopes for the children to find – a letters and sounds treasure hunt." We also hide the high-frequency words and ask the children to try and find them. For example for the word 'in', we hide lots of 'in' words inside different objects.

When we plan at the end of the session for the next day, we differentiate across each curriculum area in three ways:

1. For children who might need extra support

2. For children with English as an additional language

3. For reception age children who benefit from extra challenge.

Children are encouraged to contribute their ideas to develop a rich learning environment.

The reception group did not like a recent dinosaur builder's tray scenario, so we encouraged them to redesign it to their liking. What was interesting was their clear desire to incorporate more of their current learning of letters and sounds. They re-organised the materials in a different way, and created labels – 'Welcome' and 'No Humans Allowed'.

We aim for 100% child-initiated evidence for our early years foundation stage profiles, which supports us to keep our environment as child-led and interesting as possible.

Links to practice

- The excellent practice described opposite shows a real commitment to child-initiated learning.

- One of these commitments is shown by how they differentiate and plan for different children's needs and abilities.

- How does this work in your setting?

- Plan a new, inspiring learning experience using a child or children's interests as your starting point.

- Think about how you might plan this opportunity to suit different children and their developmental needs.

- Observe the activity and assess how well you think it goes?

There is a fine balance between giving a child just enough help and support to succeed in something they have chosen to do, and not giving enough, when there is the risk that they might give up. Succeeding in something you have set out to do is immensely valuable for children's self-esteem and self-efficacy (believing you can do it).

As well as supporting feelings and promoting language, talking through difficulties with sensitive adult support will develop children's critical thinking. What ideas do they have that might solve a problem? Could another strategy work? Effective teaching builds on these experiences. For example, children at Hindleys Preschool safely explored the view from a ladder, and then built their own with a student helper so two could climb together to see over the fence into the fields beyond.

> " Careful thought and consideration needs to be given to keeping young children safe, but this must be balanced with supporting the development of important life skills. "

Top 10 tips for being willing to 'have a go'

1. Talk about how you learn through your mistakes, and how we can get better at things with practice.

2. Notice and praise a child's hard work and effort when they are trying to do something.

3. Help children to reflect on how they managed to complete a task, what steps did they take?

4. Talk about your own experience of being nervous or 'scared' before trying something new, and how pleased you were afterwards.

5. Celebrate children's enthusiasm for what they enjoy doing and their growing confidence.

6. Be ready to support a child to carry through a challenge they have set themselves – such as putting on their shoes, pushing a straw into a carton of milk etc.

7. Do adults model making mistakes, getting stuck and finding solutions?

8. Consider how you engage in children's play. Do you follow the children's ideas and enhance their play rather than taking over?

9. Reflect back with children how they found some activities or skills difficult, but can now do them more easily. Home-make books or children's records of achievement will be helpful here.

10. Provide a variety of storybooks with a motivational element. For example, *Dear Zoo* by Rod Campbell, *Amazing Grace* by Mary Hoffman, *Frog is Frog* by Max Velthuijs or *When Pigs Fly* by Valerie Coalman.

Chapter 5:
A thoughtful approach

As children engage through **playing and exploring** (and **active learning** and **creating and thinking critically**) they will be developing learning dispositions, which will support them to continue as motivated, enthusiastic learners, able to have a go, and willing to try again if something doesn't go according to plan first time round.

As children move through their early years, there will be a gradual progression from mostly child-led opportunities and experiences for the youngest children to a balance of child-initiated learning and adult-led focused activities and support

(See the example on page 63). Engaging parents in their children's learning and allowing children to discover new skills through their mistakes will be important aspects.

The next two case studies depict different ways that parents were involved and supported in their children's learning. Good practice will mean that you take a thoughtful approach to the diverse ways in which you include parents and make links with home. This will range from a brief five-minute chat at drop-off time, to planning for a parent to introduce a cultural activity in the setting, to taking part in a shared, community event.

Study: working together with parents

Tracy Hewitt works closely with parents in her childminding practice.

One child, Amy was really not very keen on hair-washing. "Mum and I discussed this difficulty and I thought about how I might support lots of practical experiences linked to the theme of 'hair-washing and hair' in order to build Amy's confidence in this area". Tracy organised a series of small role plays using the dolls in the setting and encouraged Amy to help her brush the dolls hair, and get them ready for a party. "We talked about how we make ourselves look smart, and I remember I had my hair brushed a lot that week!". I planned some opportunities to wash doll's hair, with little bottles of shampoo, and bowls of water. This really encouraged Amy to experience the pleasure of bubbles, the lovely smells of the shampoo and most importantly to be in charge. "I also found a 'Barbie' hair-dressing head, and set up a hair-dressing area".

Although Amy still found having her hair washed difficult, these playful experiences allowed her the opportunity to talk about her experiences, and think about ways she could be more involved in taking charge of washing her own hair at home.

If we want children to develop positive dispositions, for example, being able to work in a team; friendliness; motivation; curiosity, creative thinking etc., we need to model these ourselves as practitioners and parents. The example of 'The pea fair' below is how one setting involved parents in their children's playing and exploring.

Example: The pea fair – Celebrating and sharing learning with children and their families

At Rainbow Nursery towards the end of the summer term, the head of centre, Clare, and her team organised a 'pea fair' for the first time. "This is an old-fashioned type of fair and we felt it would give us a different sort of opportunity to celebrate the end of term with the children and families we work with. We planned lots of fun mathematical activities and parents were able to see how the children really enjoyed and learnt through their play".

A starting point for the fair was to make small fabrics bags with the children using a hand-operated sewing machine. With support, children used the sewing machine themselves, choosing fabrics and decorative braid. Spare bags were sewn by one of the practitioners for any children who didn't want to make bags or happened to miss the sewing days. Dry chickpeas were spray painted gold and each person was given 10 chickpeas to put in their bag – this was in effect their 'spending money'. Parents and children baked cakes and flapjacks, and different games, activities and challenges were set up on the day. Some of the very creative ideas are detailed here:

- Small-world figures were hidden in sparkly sand in a builder's tray. Each figure had a different number of dots stuck on the bottom with tape. Children had to find one figure, count the dots, and could then exchange the number they had counted for a corresponding number of 'gold peas'.

- Skittles – the number of skittles that you knocked down could be exchanged for gold peas.

- Flapjacks and cakes cost '3 peas each'.

- Rides in the wheelbarrow, a big favourite, had to be saved up for, and cost 10 peas a go.

- Hopscotch counting – children threw a beanbag to land on one of the chalked squares with a number on it, hopped to the square and back again. Your reward was the same number of golden peas as the number on the square.

- Ten jumps on the trampoline for one gold pea.

Links to practice

Mathematics was taught here in a fun and contextual way, with everyone contributing to learning.

Opportunities to deepen the experience were planned the week after in the setting.

Some children were inspired to replicate their favourite games at home.

What ways could you involve parents in playful activities together with their children?

Example Rich outdoor play

At New River Green Children's Centre on the morning of my visit, the wide, open space in the centre of the garden had been resourced with a selection of large, hollow blocks. Practitioners had observed children who had been building and constructing indoors, and in particular, a group of boys who had been interested in exploring and combining different materials together with the blocks.

A short piece of plastic guttering was balanced on top of two blocks by several children, a third joining in to help. The children were gathering up small coloured balls, and sending them down the guttering, watching as they bounced off at the end. Their excited shouts drew other children's interest, and soon a larger group of children were involved in exploring and experimenting with rolling different balls down the gutter-run. The practitioner supported the play, standing back so he could see the whole group, but moving in closer to offer an occasional comment and question. He was sensitive to the children's explorations, letting them take the lead in deciding which direction they wanted to take their play.

After observing for a while, he went and fetched several lengths of guttering, placing them nearby. Two boys, Ade and Michael immediately began to extend the 'pipe' with the new lengths of guttering. They selected small blocks and placed these at different intervals. They discovered that the pipes had to be connected in a particular way – the balls would stop unless the

Pause for thought

- The block play has provided a wide range of diverse learning experiences.

- It is important to remember that although the children are engaged in similar play, they are all gaining and learning different ways.

- The two boys are intent on working out how to create a run that works and collaborate together to succeed.

- One child is developing her skills to join-in with a group, sometimes she struggles, but keeps trying, and practises several different ways to enter the game; by making a suggestion, by waiting and watching, by bringing some resources, and by helping another child to move a block.

- Several children seem interested in the speed of the balls movement and negotiate turns with each other to roll balls along the pipes.

- Other children are more focused on their developing friendships and social interactions.

- The practitioner skilfully facilitates all of these various levels of learning. He holds both a peripheral view of the play, and is able to 'zoom-in' as needed to support a particular interaction or difficulty, to keep the play moving along.

- Being attentive to children's interests and where they are in their learning should raise the thoughtful question: 'how else might I support this child's progress?' This could involve scheduling time for children to talk about their play and ask questions, as well as acknowledging and celebrating with a child their recent achievements.

pipes were joined one into the other from the top to the bottom of the run. They showed real determination to make this work, and were undeterred by other children joining in. They continued to explore and maintain their fascination for building the run. A little while later, several other children managed to move a very large pipe over to the play and this was added to extend the pipe length even more. This gave a whole new dimension to the play, and a great deal of excitement, as the ball disappeared through the new pipe, to reappear at the other end!

Case study – playful adult-led activities to support the transition to year one

Towards the end of the summer term, reception children at Rhodes Avenue Primary school spend time with their new, year one teacher in the classroom they will be moving to. One visit included a creative activity so that children could make their own superhero figures (small photographs of each child were supplied by the reception teacher). These figures were later displayed at the entrance of the classroom to welcome the children when they arrived at the start of term.

Any child who missed this opportunity was able to make their figure in the reception class, and a follow-up visit was planned so both reception and year one children could talk to each other and ask questions. Parents were also invited 'to pop in at the end of day to see us and say hello' to the year 1 teacher.

The reception teacher told me that the children enjoyed their visit to talk with the year 1 children: "They asked lots of questions and seemed reassured to hear about other children's experiences. I will be planning this again for next year". Several children shared some of their worries, which the year one children were able to answer and they all spent time in the playground together. Children were paired up, with older children supporting the younger children – this really helped the older children see how much they knew. Children in both classes seemed more confident after this exchange so transitions for both were supported.

Links to practice

What strategies do you have in place to support transitions between different groups? This is particularly important with the move from a more play-based approach to more formal learning. In the example above the reception and year 1 teacher used an ongoing interest in superheroes to plan a transition activity. This prompted a deeper conversation about playful learning into year 1.

Dilemmas of play

There are many levels to supporting and planning for playing and exploring for babies and young children. It raises different questions and concerns for practitioners:

- The adults role in play – when to intervene, how to support, what sorts of play and exploration should be encouraged?

- When should I stop play?

- Types of play – rough and tumble, superhero or weapon play can be particularly challenging when it is repetitive. Careful observation is needed to see where best and how to intervene – whether this is about introducing a new element, or setting a limit by joining the play yourself as a play partner.

- Planning for different ages in the same room.

- Thinking about how to facilitate different needs and include children of differing abilities. For example in the block play example on page 40, one child who had specific mobility

Pause for thought

Children make many transitions throughout the day – some of these transitions will involve the daily routine such as tidy-up or meal times or arriving and going home. Some changes will be more significant, such as the move to a different class and key person, or a family circumstance such as a new baby. Children may experience anxiety or added stress during these times, and will show this in different ways.

Careful thought will need to be given to support new children and their families settling in for the first time, and in the case of a new practitioner.

Some children may need specific planned help with regard to any concerns about their development and progress, or a particular special educational need. Key practitioners and parents will need the opportunity to discuss and plan next best steps.

needs enjoyed the challenge of a shoe-shop 'footstool', with a short slope and soft covered seat and spent time practicing different ways of getting on and off the stool.

Key points for a thoughtful approach

The practice examples in this chapter demonstrate a thoughtful approach to supporting children as they play and explore. Reflective practitioners will be thinking about some of the dilemmas linked to playing and exploring, and how best to support the babies and young children they work with. If you are a practitioner in a lead position, you will have the important role of modelling good practice – the manner in which you observe, plan and extend learning through playing and exploring sets the scene for the whole setting.

● Make time to discuss children's explorations and interests with other members of the team. If you are a lead practitioner, you could make this a priority, either informally at the end of each day, or as part of a staff meeting, and discuss and encourage others to think about how best to follow these up.

● Planning to extend children's learning through their self-chosen interests and activities may include: making alterations to the learning environment; planning a special visitor (for example, in the 'Do Dragons Exist' case study, 'Sir Percival the Knight and his dragon' came to speak to the children); facilitating an adult-led experience to support children's thinking and find out where to go next or it may involve adding a new possibility (for example, a 'dragons egg' was introduced to the play 'Do dragons exist?').

● 'Being in the moment' of children's play and experiences can be uncertain. We don't know what is going to happen next, although when we know children well we can sometimes make predictions. Good practice requires practitioners to develop their confidence and skill to 'be in the same moment', and trust the child's own learning process.

● Displays can provide an important connection for children and adults about the learning process, but it is worth thinking about how to utilise your displays – displays for children need to be interactive, at child height and offer possibilities for children to input their own ideas, work and comments. Displays for adults need to be clear, welcoming and attractive. How will you make links between children's playing and exploring and the learning taking place?

● Your national early years framework will detail what your statutory requirements are – (be clear about what these are), but it will also leave room for you to make decisions, imaginatively and creatively, about how to plan and support babies and young children's playing and exploring.

● Pre-determined 'topics' or 'themes' only work when they act a broad outline for children's own fascinations, personal experiences and interests. They should never take priority over children's self-initiated 'topics' of interest, or the challenges they have set themselves.

● Mentor a less experienced practitioner or student to support play and exploring in appropriate ways – watching, listening, and intervening with sensitivity. Take time to discuss possible next steps for learning together, and how this way of 'teaching' is also developing the characteristics of effective learning.

● Be thoughtful both individually and as a team (if you are in a group setting), about the sorts of Interactions and interventions that really seem to help play and exploring to continue.

● Consider how you involve parents in their children's learning. Engage colleagues in a discussion about how well this works at the moment. Are there ways in which you could improve this, and support playing and exploring at home?

> *Activities and experiences reflect the children's curiosity and fascinations, and planning becomes a two-way process between teachers and children.*

- Getting out and about and visiting other settings, as well as attending training and talks will help you to reflect on your practice and gain inspiration and new ideas.

Celebrate with children and other practitioners the process and success's of learning through playing and exploring. Good practice takes time to grow and develop, and an enabling environment for play will support both adults and children learning together.

Did dragons exist?

In this final case study, a creative question linked to the children's interests in knights, castles, princess's and dragons inspired new learning and deep thinking. Children's creativity, interests and questions are the starting point for the Cornerstones creative curriculum which Carcroft Primary School follow.

This thoughtful approach allowed the teachers to plan imaginatively for adult-led, focused activities together with plenty of time for open-ended child-led play and exploration. Children were enthused to write and incorporate their knowledge of phonics into the play.

If we look at this learning story of the children's involvement in finding out if dragons existed, what can we see in relation to their playing and exploring?

Finding out and exploring

The children are provided with compelling opportunities to find out and explore. Activities and experiences reflect the children's curiousity and fascinations, and planning becomes a two-way process between teachers and children. They use all of their senses to engage in the different experiences, and in particular, enjoy finding out about the bearded dragons. Children then combine and use these diverse experiences creatively in playing with what they know.

Playing with what they know

Rich opportunities for small world, role play and an exciting visitor – the 'real knight and his dragon', inspired children to explore, develop and take on different roles in their play. New vocabulary was introduced and practiced; dramatic story-making provided the raw material for later writing, and imaginative stories and non-fiction texts supported this. The children also represented their experiences through expressive arts and design by creating models, sculptures, drawing and painting.

Being willing to 'have a go'

The teachers actively sought children's collaboration and ideas, and were open to how the play might develop. This signals to the children a clear message 'it's alright to try new things, take a risk and learn through trial and error'. The children were encouraged to initiate their own activities, building their confidence to 'have a go'. They show a 'can-do' attitude as they care for the dragon egg, and the dragon baby when it hatches.

CASE STUDY – starting points

The interest developed with a question (something to think about): 'Did dragons exist?'. The provocation was given to the children (aged 5+) by their teachers as part of their creative curriculum, aiming to get children to talk together, think creatively, hypothesise and problem solve. What could be the possible answers to this question?

The play developed as the children became more interested in castles, knights and dragons. It included making imaginative stories using the small world castle and figures and building castles and lots of talk: 'raise the draw bridge' using the wooden blocks. The children took on the parts of the characters they had created and gave directions and orders: "Pull

up the drawbridge there's a dragon coming". They played collaboratively, concentrating for long periods of time and becoming very involved in the stories.

The teachers recorded what the children did and said using photographs and making notes and used this to plan the next steps.

The teachers invited Sir Percival the Knight and his dragon to visit the class (the knight was a member of staff) to provoke more thinking and develop the children's ideas about knights, castles and dragons. They told the story of the knight and his dragon and spoke with the children.

The conversation between them and the children developed with the children asking lots of questions. This led to even more ideas, inspiring the children, who in the following days became engaged in role play, building a castle and finding clothes to wear as well as preparing a banquet.

The role play grew after the knight and dragons visit – with children creating their own stories and becoming knights, princesses, kings and queens. They made the props they needed like the castle, swords, horses, banquet food and brought in dressing up outfits from home. The children recreated things from the stories they had heard, the discussions they had with each other and the teachers and the significant moments that had been planned. The children's ideas were supported by the teachers giving them the time, space and opportunities to construct their thinking and follow their interest. Planning was based on observing the children as they were playing and involved in conversations.

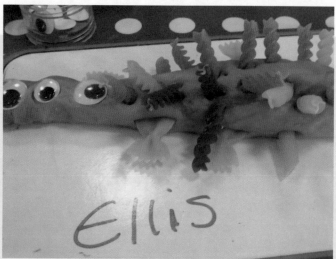

Some 'real' dragons came to school along with snakes and spiders and the children began to look more closely at other types of dragons. They found out about the lives, habits and make up of bearded dragons. They were able to touch them, hold them and take a very close look which led to much discussion both at the time and afterwards.

In the following days and weeks they recreated the experience through their drawing, painting, collage, clay, dough and writing.

CASE STUDY – finding the dragon's egg

One morning the children found a dragon egg underneath a cushion where it was warm. The dragon egg was 'planted' to provoke the children's responses and language as well as getting them to think about how it got there. 'What do we do next? How do we look after the egg?'. It stirred their imagination and furthered discussion.

Looking after the dragon egg progresses over several days, after it had hatched the children decided that they needed to care for it by wrapping it in a blanket, reading stories and involving him in their play.

The adults supported all of their ideas and gave them the responsibility of what to do, when and how. The children shared their thoughts about the dragons care in a collaborative partnership, which included negotiation, planning and thinking ahead – they took this role very seriously.

The original question that had been posed by the teachers was: 'Did dragons exist?'. They offered the question to the children as a starting point for creative thinking, active learning and play and exploration and then supported the children's growing ideas and interest by following their lead and adding in memorable, planned moments

to extend their thinking and learning. The whole experience was co-constructed in partnership between the children and the teachers with a balance of child-initiated ideas and adult-led/focused activities resulting in some deep and meaningful thinking and learning. The children were inspired to write about their experiences.

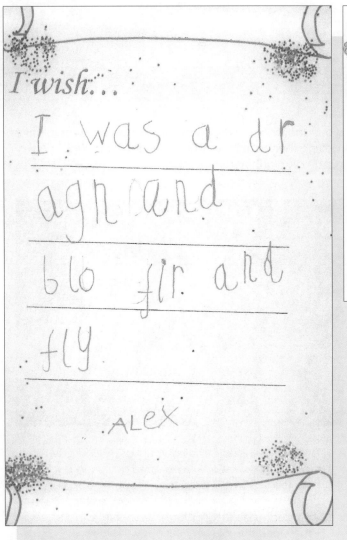

I wish...

I was a dr
agn and
blo fir and
fly

ALex

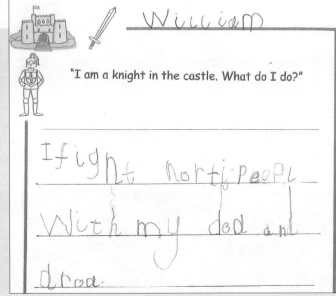

"I am a knight in the castle. What do I do?"

Ifight norti peepl
With my dad and
droa.

The children, boys and girls, were keen to write and saw this as a natural extension of their quest to find out if dragons existed.

The teachers has made sure that the writing tasks were embedded into realistic activities like invitations to the banquet, wishes and mystical stories as well as job descriptions of what a knight, princess, king, queen or dragon should do.

Writing happened anywhere and at any time.

'Did Dragons Exist?' and how this links to the aspects of playing and exploring

If we look at this learning story of the children's involvement in finding out if dragons existed, what can we see in relation to their playing and exploring?

Finding out and exploring	Playing with what they know	Being willing to 'have a go'
The children are provided with compelling opportunities to find out and explore throughout the whole project. They are curious, show particular interests and engage in a variety of open-ended activities. They use all of their senses to engage in the different experiences, and enjoy finding out about real dragons.	There are rich possibilities to represent experiences throughout. The starting point for this learning experience was an invitation for the children to take on a role in their play, as co-investigators! Children were able to develop the play and act out their experiences with others. They represent these experiences in many different ways, through the role play and writing about the experience.	Children engaged in new experiences through their role-play and by the exciting introduction of real dragons. They enjoyed the challenge of helping to hatch the egg, showing a 'can do' attitude. The teachers model positive dispositions for example to investigate, take risks, and support the children to reflect on their experiences, and form a narrative about their play.

Appendices

CHARACTERISTICS OF EFFECTIVE TEACHING AND LEARNING

Playing and exploring – engagement	Active learning – motivation	Creating and thinking Critically – thinking
Finding out and exploring	**Being involved and concentrating**	**Having their own ideas**
Babies and children are curious about objects, events and people.	Babies and children are able to sustain a focus on their activity for a period of time.	Children think of and have their own ideas.
They use their senses to explore the world around them.	They show high levels of energy and fascination.	They find ways to solve problems.
They engage in open-ended activity.	They are not easily distracted.	They work out and discover new ways to do things.
Babies and children show particular interest in certain things, for example exploring water or sand.	They pay attention to details, for example, spending time watching a ladybird crawl across a leaf.	For example – a child struggles to put their coat on. They place their coat on the floor and experiment by lying down and sliding first one hand through a sleeve and then the other. They stand up with the coat on, delighted!
Playing with what they know	**Keeping on trying**	**Making links**
Children pretend objects are things from their own experience – a plastic bottle becomes a drill.	Babies and children are able to persist and continue with an activity when challenges occur.	Children make links and discover patterns in their experiences.
They represent their experiences in play, i.e. a child who has had a birthday recently plays at making birthday cakes with the play-dough and cuts up bits of straw for 'candles'.	They believe that more effort or a different strategy may well pay off.	They are willing and able to predict.
A child takes on a role during play – 'I'm the daddy'.	They are able to bounce back after a set-back or difficulty.	They test out their ideas.
They act out experiences with other people.		They develop ideas of groupings, sequence and cause and effect. For example 'when the gutter is higher, I think my cars will roll faster!'.
Being willing to 'have a go'	**Enjoying achieving what they set out to do**	**Choosing ways to do things**
Children initiate activities.	Children show satisfaction when they meet a goal they have set for themselves.	Children plan and make decisions about how to approach a task, solve a problem or reach a goal.
They set and seek their own challenges.	They are proud of **how** they have accomplished something, not just the end result.	They check to see how well their activities are going.
Children have a 'can do' attitude.	They enjoy meeting challenges for their own sake, not for an external reward or praise.	They will switch strategies to suit.
They are willing to take a risk, engage in a new experience and learn by trial and error.		They review how well the strategy works, i.e. when I lifted the gutter higher, my car did go very fast!'.

Compiled by Anni McTavish, with reference to Development Matters 2012 by Helen Moylet and Nancy Stewart, Early Education – free to download from http://www.foundationyears.org.uk/

CHARACTERISTICS OF EFFECTIVE LEARNING – PLAYING AND EXPLORING

	Aspects	Did you see this happening?	A unique child – observing **how** a child learns What did you see/hear? How was this happening?
Playing and exploring – engagement			
Finding out and exploring	• Babies and children are curious about objects, events and people. • They use their senses to explore the world around them. • They engage in open-ended activity. • Babies and children show particular interest in certain things.		
Playing with what they know	• Children pretend objects are things from their own experience – a plastic bottle becomes a drill. • They represent their experiences in play, e.g. reenact a birthday. • A child takes on a role during play. • They act out experiences with other people.		
Being willing to 'have a go'	• Children initiate activities. • They set and seek their own challenges. • Children have a 'can do' attitude. • They are willing to take a risk, engage in a new experience and learn by trial and error.		
What could we do next?			

Adapted from original pro-forma devised by Di Chilver

The Balance Cake Recipe

(A great 'have a go' activity and encourages early maths skills)

Used with kind permission from Anna Ephgrave, from her book *The Reception Year in Action*, published by David Fulton/Routledge, 2011 UK.

The aim of this simple recipe is to create your own visual recipe – using photographs of the children demonstrating each step of the way. You will need a set of plastic, 'rocker scales', available from early years suppliers, a mixing bowl and wooden spoon.

1. On the scales balance 1 egg with flour.

2. Put the flour in the bowl.

3. On the scales balance the egg with sugar.

4. Put the sugar in the bowl.

5. On the scales balance the egg with butter.

6. Put the butter in the bowl.

7. Put the egg in the bowl.

8. Mix it up!

9. Put the mixture in a big cake tin or in little cake tins!

10. Cook at 190°C for 15 minutes.

Playdough – uncooked
(as mentioned on page 11)

1 ½ cups salt
1 ½ tablespoons vegetable cooking oil
1 tablespoon cream of tartar
2 cups boiling water
3 cups plain flour
Food colour optional

Mix the first four ingredients together in a large bowl and then add flour.

Stir well until the mixture leaves the sides of the bowl.

Add more flour if the mixture seems too sticky, then turn out and knead.

Store in plastic bag/Tupperware in fridge or cool cupboard, will last at least a week.

Playdough – cooked
(as mentioned on page 11)

3 cups plain flour
1 ½ cups salt
3 tablespoons cooking oil
1 tablespoon cream of tartar
3 cups water
Food colouring

Mix ingredients in large saucepan and cook over medium heat until mixture
pulls away from sides and becomes play-dough consistency.

Knead until cool – this is lovely to do with children while it's still warm!

It will keep for 2-3 months in a plastic container.

Add oil scents, spices, hot chocolate powder for 'chocolate' play-dough, glitter, (not sequins, as they can be very sharp.)

Please note – as with all cooking activities, check that children are not allergic to any
of the ingredients, and do not use for children 18 months or under, who are still exploring by mouth.

Cooked Corn flour Jelly
(as mentioned on page 11)

2-3 cups (add more for a thicker mixture) corn flour

2-3 cups cold water and a 'just-boiled' kettle of very hot water

Medium-large saucepan & wooden spoon

Food colouring

Mix the corn flour with the cold water until you have got rid of all the lumps
(either mix in a large bowl or bucket, or a saucepan if you have access to a stove).

Add the 'just boiled' water stirring continuously, and the mixture should begin to thicken.

Alternatively, once you have added the hot water, bring the mixture slowly to boiling on the
stove, stirring continuously to prevent sticking – the mixture should quickly thicken into a paste-like sauce.

Add food colouring if using.

Allow to cool thoroughly before using.

Will keep for several days in fridge, but will get runnier over time.
(This mixture gets very hot while cooking, please take care!)

The corn flour jelly can be used in lots of different ways:

Divide into 4 separate pots and add different paint colours to create your own finger paints

Add to a builders tray with moss, pebbles and fir cones to create an imaginative play landscape for small world

Add to small bowls or a builders tray for young children to explore the sensory and mark-making possibilities

Please note – as with all cooking activities, check that children are not allergic to any of the
ingredients, and do not use for children 18 months or under, who are still exploring by mouth.

References

Resources

Children's Scrapstore PlayPod Project
(http://www.playpods.co.uk).

Development Matters 2012 (can be downloaded from
www.foundationyears.org.uk).

Eco Schools: further information about the Eco schools/Green
Flag initiative can be found on the following site. The different
countries in Great Britain have their own 'home' site linked to
Eco schools (http://www.eco-schools.org).

Health and Safety Executive – Children's play and leisure
– Promoting a balanced approach (http://www.hse.gov.uk/
entertainment/childs-play-statement.htm).

*Developing Play for Under Threes – ideas and information about
creating treasure baskets and heuristic play collections*
by Hughes, A. M., 2nd Edition, Routledge, London (2010).

References

Bruce, T. (2001) *Learning through play: babies Toddlers and the
Foundation Years*, p.117, Hodder and Stoughton London.

Bronson, M. (2000) *Self-regulation in Early Childhood: Nature
and Nurture*, Guilford Press, New York.

Brooker, L. (2010) p.27 and p.37, 'Learning to Play in a Cultural
Context' in *Play and Learning in the Early Years*, (Broadhead, P.,
Howard, J. and Wood, E. 2010) Sage Publications Ltd, 2010, London.

Carr, M. & Claxton, G. (March 2004) A Framework for teaching
learning: the dynamics of disposition, *Early Years*, Volume 4, No 1.

Development Matters, 2012 (www.foundationyears.org.uk).

Dowling, M. (2005) Supporting Young Children's Sustained
Shared Thinking – An Exploration, Training Materials Early
Education (http://www.early-education.org.uk).

Department for Education (DfE) (2012) Statutory Framework
for the Early Years Foundation Stage, London, crown copyright
(www.foundationyears.org.uk).

Ephgrave, A. (2011) *The Reception Year in Action*, David Fulton.

EPPE – Effective Provision of Pre-School Education Project
(http://eppe.ioe.ac.uk/eppe/eppeintro.htm).

Goldschmied, E. and Jackson, S. p.97, 2nd Ed (2004) *People
Under Three, Young Children in Day Care*, Routledge, London.

Health and Safety Executive 2012 – new statement.

Holland, P. (2003) *We don't play with Guns Here – War, Weapon
and Superhero Play in Early Years*, Open University Press, England.

Hughes, A. (2006) *Developing Play for Under Threes*,
David Fulton Publishers, London.

Hutt et al. (1989) referenced in Free Play in Early Childhood,
a literature review, NCB, 2007.

Lindon, J. (2012) *Planning for Effective Early Learning*,
Practical Pre-School Books, London.

McTavish, A. (2008) *50 Exciting Ideas for Superheroes
and popular Culture*, Lawrence Educational UK
(www.lawrenceeducational.co.uk/nal).

Mark Making Matters (2008) National Strategies
(available at www.foundationyears.org.uk).

Moyles, J. (2010) *The Excellence of Play* 3rd Edition,
Open University Press, England.

References

Moylett, H. and Stewart, N. (2012) *Understanding the revised Early Years Foundation Stage*, Early Education (http://www.early-education.org.uk).

Nutbrown, C., Hannon, P., and Morgan, A. (2005) *Early literacy work with families*, SAGE Publications, London (The ORIM project).

O'Hare, N. (2006) 'All Ears' article – The Things That Matter, The National Literacy Trust, London (http://www.literacytrust.org.uk/talk_to_your_baby/news/1648_all_ears).

ORIM – more information about the 'Keeping It Real' project (ORIM can be found here http://www.real-online.group.shef.ac.uk/).

Pound, L. (2005) *How Children Learn*, Practical Pre-School Books, London.

Rubin (1983) in Bruce, T. (2005) p.191, *Early Childhood Education* 3rd Ed, Hodder Arnold.

Tickell, C. (2011) The Early Years: Foundations for life, health and learning, An Independent Report on the Early Years Foundation Stage to Her Majesty's Government, London: DfE crown copyright (http://media.education.gov.uk/MediaFiles/B/1/5/%7BB15EFF0D-A4DF-4294-93A1-1E1B88C13F68%7DTickell%20review.pdf).

Supporting Children learning English as an additional language (2007 Primary National Strategies) (http://www.foundationyears.org.uk/2011/10/supporting-children-learning-english-as-an-additional-language/).

Acknowledgements

My warm thanks to all the settings, managers, practitioners and childminders, parents and children who have contributed to this book:

- Pastures Way Nursery School, Luton

- Wiggly Jigglers and Jasmine Pasch, Rich Mix, Shoreditch

- Carcroft Primary School, Doncaster

- College Green Nursery School and Services, London Borough of Brent

- Hindleys Pre-School, Leicestershire

- New River Green Children's Centre, London Borough of Islington

- Sheringham Nursery School and Children's Centre, London Borough of Newham

- Rainbow Nursery, Kentish Town, London Borough of Camden

- Glasgow City Council EAL Peripatetic Response Team

- Rhodes Avenue Primary School, London Borough of Haringey.

Special mention goes to Jan Allen, Sue Moss and all at Pastures Way Nursery School who welcomed me so warmly, and gave permission for many of the photographs and case studies.

Final thanks to Di Chilvers and Helen Moylett for lots of inspiring conversations along the way.